SOILED COPY
sold at a reduced price

SCHOOL DAYS AND STEAM DAYS

'A good read that brought back memories of my pre-war railway observations and travel, especially on the Bootle Branch. Trainspotters were not as numerous then. Sadly young trainspotters are now a vanished species.'
The late John Gahan, formerly 'Linesman' in *Meccano Magazine* and author of *Rails to Port and Starboard* and others

'Once I started to read it, I could not put it down.'
The late Jim Peden, respected North West photographer of industrial and BR steam

'A brilliant story, which I thoroughly enjoyed, capturing the atmosphere of the trainspotting era. I even relived the magic of copping my one and only "Mickey" namer.'
Peter Kelly, former editor of *The Railway Magazine* and *Steam Railway*

SCHOOL DAYS AND STEAM DAYS

The trainspotting adventures
of Paul Carr

Barry Allen

SLP

Silver Link Publishing

First published in 2012

Printed and bound in the Czech Republic

British Library Cataloguing in Publication Data

A catalogue record for this book is available from the British Library.

ISBN 978 1 85794 395 5

Silver Link Publishing Ltd
The Trundle
Ringstead Road
Great Addington
Kettering
Northants NN14 4BW

Tel/Fax: 01536 330588
email: sales@nostalgiacollection.com
Web: www.nostalgiacollection.com

Front cover picture: At Crewe in the late 1950s hordes of young spotters watch intently as rebuilt 'Royal Scot' No 46101 *Royal Scots Grey* runs into the station with a special. This engine often appeared at various locations in the North West and was not the most popular member of the class. During the summer school holidays BR officials periodically banned spotters from Crewe station, as they frequently outnumbered passengers. Common sense eventually prevailed – like King Canute, they could not hold back the tide! *E. M. Johnson*

ACKNOWLEDGEMENTS

Special thanks go to Eddie Johnson, Brian Green, David Wilcock, the late Jim Peden and the late John Gahan for their assistance in producing this book, and to all those who provided photographs, thus enhancing it. Thanks also to all the footplate crews who provided endless hours of free entertainment, and to railway preservationists everywhere, 'or keeping our trainspotting memories alive.

All the author's profits from book sales will go to UK 'way preservation, and also to the upkeep of a special vay carriage for the disabled.

Allen
ool

CONTENTS

Foreword by David Wilcock   7
Foreword by Eddie Johnson   11
Preface   13

1   The footbridge   15
2   Crewe   30
3   Shed bunking   51
4   Southern steam   66
5   Chester, Shrewsbury –
    and Wolverhampton?   84
6   Carlisle   105
7   Preston   117
8   Manchester, Leeds and York   136

Postscript   159
Glossary   160

'Merchant Navy' 'Pacific' No 35028 *Clan Line* – since preserved – wai
patiently with an express at Waterloo station in August 1966. Spotte
peer curiously into the cab, while a young photographer moves down th
platform in search of other subjects. The plume of steam from the safe
valves signifies that *Clan Line* has a full head of steam for the task ahea
All Bulleid 'Pacifics' were built with electric lighting, which many drive
considered a great step forward. One wonders why a similar feature wa
not incorporated into the new BR Standards introduced in 1951. *Gec
Parrish*

FOREWORD
by
David Wilcock
Founding editor, *Steam Railway* and *Steam World* magazines

To all intents and purposes, the cult of 'trainspotting' died several decades ago. Even at once bustling railway hubs like Crewe or Doncaster, it's rare today to see enthusiasts gathered in groups on platform ends, fervently writing numbers in their notebooks as they once did. The handful who still do are very much a minority, though society still dwells on its traditional, long-held if somewhat jaundiced view, that all railway enthusiasts are geeks or anoraks. Actually we're not – but it's hard to escape being tarred by that brush.

How times have changed. Back in the 1950s and 1960s you were odd if you *weren't* a trainspotter! The newly nationalised British Railways inherited more than 20,000 steam locomotives in 1948, ranked into hundreds of different classes, and between 1951 and 1960 was busy building another 1,000 new locomotives, every single one of them neatly listed and laid out in Ian Allan's annually published bible of steam, the *ABC Combined Volume*. Simply put, there was never a more vibrant, more pulsating time to get hooked on railways, and if ever there was an invitation to the nation's schoolboys, the *Combined Volume* was it. It effectively said: 'OK, lads – here they all are – now go out and spot them!' And hundreds of thousands of schoolboys did exactly that.

Long before phrases like 'soap opera' or 'computer game' entered our lexicon, lads –often as young as six or seven in short (and sometimes long) trousers and frequently in school uniform, complete with caps, took root on bridges and platforms on every main line (and many branch lines) across the country, in eager anticipation of what might come steaming by next. It was an age in which kids did pretty much what their parents told them to do, and 'the bobby on the beat' was a man to be respected, or even feared (he could clip a cheeky kid around the ear without fear of being sued for assault). But for the ardent trainspotter, the parental instruction to 'be home for tea by 5.30' was a tough (and quite unreasonable!) one to obey!

My mother was always content in the knowledge that if I wasn't at home I was 'just down the road' glued to one or another railway bridge near our house on the 'suburban' stretch of the West Coast Main Line between Euston and Watford. If she had known that on many occasions, her eight-year-old son wasn't actually 'just down the road' at all, but 'bashing' different engine sheds more than 30 miles away on the other side of London, she would have had fits.

Trainspotting in the post-war steam era of the 1950s and '60s was for many nothing less than an addiction, and it is in this very special, happy window of history that my good friend and lifetime steam enthusiast Barry Allen has pitched this book.

Although the stories are by definition fiction, they're closely based on Barry's own recollections and experiences with spotting pals during his 'growing up' years in the Merseyside area, and have a tangible sense of reality about them.

They might be 'the trainspotting adventures of Paul Carr', but they're an echo of the trainspotting adventures of David Wilcock and, I don't doubt, you yourself, and everyone who you know as well.

Didn't every group of trainspotting pals have a slightly awkward 'fat kid' like Tubby Hughes, who was always eating, and a fount-of-all-railway-knowledge like Philip Wood? Who didn't come to feel the fatal stab of that frantic angry 'Oi!' that was bellowed at you from across the shed yard by the running foreman or shed master – so often the opening line in the swift process of ejection from the engine sheds where, as schoolboys, we routinely trespassed? Who didn't scribble 'I died here waiting for 46102 'Black Watch" (or some other rare beast) on bridge parapets, or posters at stations, or shout 'Ruddy stink!' or 'Scrap it!' at the common-as-muck locomotives that we'd seen at least 'a million' times before?

It may not be prudent or fashionable today to admit that you were ever a trainspotter (or even a railway enthusiast). You may even have shut it out of your psyche, and are in denial, in consideration of the ribbing you might get from friends and colleagues. Don't be – I guarantee that this sentimental journey will take you right back to those happy, grimy, halcyon times, and remind you just how bustlingly good they really were.

At Speke Junction shed on 9 February 1958, four different classes of goods locomotives can be seen; from left to right they are Midland 4F, 'Super D', 'WD' and Stanier 8F. The nose of the prototype 'Deltic' peeps out of the gloom, while a Derby Lightweight DMU awaits fuel. On the extreme right, in the adjacent siding, stands one of Speke's allocation of four diesel shunters introduced by the LMS in 1939. *W.A. Brown*

FOREWORD
by
Eddie Johnson

The pastime of trainspotting holds a very dear place in the hearts and souls of such as myself, who, having achieved the status of 'senior citizen', look back with fond memories to our early youth and that magic decade of the 1950s when engine numbers and names were our meat and drink. Though lambasted and satirised by the media, the trainspotter was a unique being.

Barry Allen, Liverpool born and bred, has created a splendid group of fictional youngsters, all bonded together by their common interest – trains. Reading through Barry's manuscript, I felt an almost immediate empathy with Paul Carr, Tubby, Badger, Philip and Pearson. Mr Barlow ('old Barlow') – the stern teacher – became to me Mr Peers, Mr Avery and Mr Berry, fierce martinets at my old secondary school in Ardwick, here in Manchester.

Daydreaming at St Gregory's was not a thing to be taken lightly. Care had to be exercised when snatching glances out of the third-floor window to gaze on sights such as 'Scots', 'Patriots' and 'Black Fives' wending their way into and out of Manchester's London Road station, which brought welcome relief from Mr Peers's endless war stories or Mr Avery's maniacal board-duster throwing. Mr Barlow seemed quite benevolent by their standards!

And so I accompanied our Liverpudlian schoolboys on their various trips, to Crewe – what memories lie there! – to York, Carlisle, Preston, Chester, Shrewsbury and London, where even a 4.30am departure was not enough to stifle unbridled youthful enthusiasm! To the teenagers on the 1950s the world was a much bigger place than it appears today. To Philip and his friends, Waterloo and Victoria must have seemed like the far side of the moon. What strange monsters the Bulleid 'Pacifics' must have looked to lads weaned on LMS 'Pacifics' and 'Jubilees'!

Paul's cycle ride to Speke engine shed had special poignancy for me and, I suspect, for many other ex-spotters who had no other mode of transport. Trafford Park, Heaton Mersey and Longsight were all in reach of my youthful home – just as Speke and Edge Hill were for Paul Carr and his friends. But our bikes had other uses as we found once when bunking the shed in Northampton – by standing on the crossbar we could gain extra height to clamber over the shed wall!

But Barry's story, a 'ripping yarn' in every sense of the word, is more than just about locomotives, trains and railways. Woven in and around their passion is their attitude to their peers, to girlfriends, their families and even to sex. I have read little else from those halcyon days that has brought back such profound memories, and given me such pleasure.

Fifty years on, members of class 5A's trainspotting gang – John Burnett, Philip Ebsworth and the author – reunite as OAPs. If any former classmate had suggested that we would meet up again half a century later, I would have thought them insane. Yet here we are, still steam enthusiasts, with endless recollections of those halcyon days. How lucky we were to have experienced such moments. *Kevin O'Toole*

PREFACE

Trainspotting was an addiction that produced countless British Railways employees, and has contributed to the success of the steam preservation movement. Even today, we can still witness main-line steam. I suggest that the building of 'A1' No 60163 *Tornado* would not have taken place without the help of numerous former spotters who financed its manufacture. Local communities and businesses now benefit from the revenue generated by the numerous visitors to preserved railways throughout the UK. Yes, the trainspotter has played an unsung role in shaping the current tourist map.

Although this story is pure fiction, some of the events portrayed are based on actual occurrences experienced by the writer during this period, and the classes of locomotives mentioned could usually be found at the stated locations. As the story is primarily written to recapture the atmosphere of trainspotting, certain liberties have been taken with timetable information, especially at Waterloo, and in no way should this document be referred to on a factual basis. You will note that I have, on occasions, used the names and numbers of steam locomotives preserved by individuals/societies, preserved railways or the National Railway Museum, and these are asterisked (*). Local trainspotting language is used throughout, and a Glossary can be found at the end of the book should you require clarification.

This story is dedicated to all who stood in the cold, wind and rain, anxious for another cop, and to the memory of my good friend David Ogwin, who accompanied me on many of the outings described.

THE SPOTTER
by
Paul Carr

A trainspotter's dream is to travel to Crewe,
Or York or Bristol, any will do;
There he'll watch and wait for trains,
Hoping of course that they all bear names.
Clinging to his book with pen in hand,
He'll travel for numbers all over the land;
Given the chance he'll be round a shed,
Or clamber aboard a footplate instead.
A good mixer is he with plenty of tales –
He'll chatter away while watching the rails.
A pulled-off signal he will immediately spot
And, after a brief interval, begin to jot,
A smile on his face, often a wave,
Experiencing magic, moments to save.
So when you see a spotter now and again,
Remember his pleasure at seeing your train.

'Carr, does this constitute two night's homework?
Please see me. BARLOW 6/10'

I
THE FOOTBRIDGE

Paul was daydreaming, the teacher's voice a dull drone, increasing his boredom. Fantasies continued. A 'Princess' locomotive was reaching the curve at Edge Hill; soon she would be storming the gradient leading to Wavertree. He could smell her, oil and steam striving valiantly to break the monotony of his tutor's voice. Autumn sunlight filtered through the window, and he wished he was elsewhere, preferably Crewe, or any other location where he could watch trains.

Yes, trains – his mind returned to Edge Hill. She was rattling her way up the gradient, fifteen coaches and just behind time.

'Wake up, Carr.'

Old Barlow was giving him a long look, and he braced himself for the sequel.

'Carr, will you repeat what I've been talking about for the last five minutes?'

He stood up. 'Er, sunspots, Sir.' Pritchard's whisper, gratefully received.

'Ah, it appears you have been listening after all. Would you mind explaining their theory?'

'Well, Sir…' He was guessing now and everybody knew his face smarted as he stumbled deeper into confusion, adding words that had vaguely registered during the preceding minutes.

'Carr, it appears that you've not been listening at all. No doubt your mind's on the 2.30 from Crewe.'

Laughter echoed around the classroom, increasing his embarrassment.

'Carr, if I'd asked you to name the type of engine hauling

the 2.30, then no doubt you'd know the answer. However, we are talking about sunspots, I'd appreciate your attention Stay behind after class, will you?'

Paul Carr sat down. There would be no trainspotting for him after school, he sullenly contemplated – it would have to wait until later.

Paul learned all about sunspots and the Sun's magnetic field, his concentration interrupted by the sound of a chime whistle heralding the arrival of a 'Britannia' 'Pacific' on Birmingham to Liverpool express, prompting the class spotters to exchange glances. 'Britannias' were infrequent visitors, and a buzz of excitement rippled around the room

The London to Liverpool main line lay approximately a quarter of a mile from the school, a lure for the district trainspotters, who assembled on the public footbridge spanning the tracks. Paul was the most ardent, spending most of his time on the footbridge steps. His father had always blamed himself for his son's addiction, having taken his infant son to Edge Hill station, later encouraging him to play with trains. Mrs Carr was adamant: it was his fault that the lad went trainspotting when he should be studying or enjoying healthier pursuits, a point often brought up during arguments.

Philip Wood was waiting for Paul when he finally left school a little after 5.00pm, thanks to some lines from old Barlow. Philip spoke first, his cheerful face breaking into smile as he greeted his disgruntled pal.

'Just thought I'd let you know that "Patriot" *Lord Rathmore* was on the 4.17 Birmingham. Oh, and *Prince Louise* was on the 4.10.'

'*Lord Rathmore*? She doesn't pay us many visits. I bet Tubby Hughes copped her. Anything else?'

'No apart from some "Mickeys". How many lines did you get?'

'Thirty. You know old Barlow – it's always lines. I'd sooner have the cane. Been waiting long?'

'About ten minutes. I thought you'd be out about five.

16

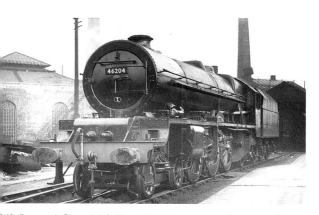

LMS 'Princess' Class 4-6-2 No 46204 *Princess Louise* is seen at Crewe Works on 24 January 1954. She was withdrawn in October 1961, not long after Paul and his friends spotted her. *Frank Hornby*

'You going to the bridge tonight, Phil?' Paul hoped for an affirmative answer from his favourite chum. Philip's father was a top link engine driver at Edge Hill shed. Some lads had all the luck!

'Do you know what the "Brit" was on the Birmingham, Phil?' Paul had been meaning to ask this question since they met.

'Yes, my Dad was driving her, that's why we received a long whistle. He always does that when he comes through just to let me know he's nearly home, and to tell Mum to put the kettle on.'

'And no doubt to let you know he's driving a "Brit",' interrupted Paul.

'Oh, that as well. Anyway, it was *Byron*. I know you've seen her.'

'Ruddy stink!' blurted Paul. 'Why can't the London Midland Region receive some different ones?'

Philip looked thoughtful. 'My Dad likes "Brits", but he

prefers a rebuilt "Patriot".

'What's his favourite class? I bet it's a "Lizzie" o
"Semi".'

'Aye, you're right, providing they steam. Mind you, h

'Britannia' 'Pacific' No 70031 *Byron* – 'Ruddy stink!' – at Crewe South she
on 10 December 1961. *The late J. M. Tolson, courtesy of Frank Hornby*

Philip's father was a top link engine driver at Edge Hill shed and liked th
'Brits'. This one is No 70048 *The Territorial Army 1908-1958*, photographe
at Edge Hill on 5 April 1963. *John Corkill*

ays a good "Black Five" will pull practically anything.'

'I like the Great Western "Castles" myself – they can't
alf shift.'

'Well, I'll let you know when one comes through Mossley
ill,' grinned his pal.

'That'll be the day. Still, it would make a change from
yron.' Paul's voice reflected a forlorn wish. 'What was your
ad driving yesterday?' he continued.

'Have you seen that new "Jubilee" that's knocking
round?'

They separated at the end of the road, Paul proceeding
a the entry wall, alongside the main line. Should a train
aterialise, he could easily scramble up – a satisfying
hought. He arrived home somewhat disappointed that there
ad been no need to test his climbing abilities. His father
as in the front garden mending the fence, accompanied
y the family pet Buster, a mongrel of dubious parentage.
ursing a scratched finger, his father paused before giving
im a frosty reception.

'Your mother's got your tea on.' It was difficult going
ow, as the dog's welcome slowed his progress. 'Anyway,
ou're late – been adding to your collection?' He paused.
You can help me in the garden after tea – that is, if you
aven't got any other plans.' He knew the answer before it
ame.

'I would, Dad, but I promised to meet Philip at the
ridge.'

That ruddy bridge, his father thought. What's the use,
e lad's train mad. 'Well, you can help your mother with the
ashing up,' he added in a peeved manner.

Paul entered the house, threw his bag on a chair and sat
own at the table. His mother was, as usual, over the stove.

'What's for tea, Mum?'

'Sausage and mash, and eat it slowly – you're no sooner
ome before you're out again. Typical of you to say "What's
r tea, Mum" instead of "Hello, Mum. Had a good day?"'

Paul took the rebuke in good grace and re-greeted his

mother. Soon they were all round the table apart from hi sister, Joan, who, being a hairdresser, often worked late. Joe Paul's brother, had left home two years earlier to join th Royal Air Force. He'd done well and was hoping for furthe promotion.

'How did school go today? Don't forget your chemistr book – you left it on the sideboard this morning.' His mothe chattered away, not noticing the dog's eyes boring into he back as she disappeared into the kitchen, only to return i equal voice carrying a Madeira cake. 'I met Mrs Johnson th other day – you know, the woman with the funny eye.'

'No I don't,' muttered Paul's father, eyeing the cake.

'You know, Norman, her eldest girl got into trouble.'

'Oh, *that* Mrs Johnson,' he nodded, still puzzled. Pau was all ears.

'You get on with your meal, young man,' said his mothe 'Anyway, her Tommy is hoping to sit the GCE in Art. Isn he in the same class as you, Paul?'

'Yes, but he's good at art – I'm not. No chance of m taking it.'

'You should practise drawing trains. Heaven knows yo should be good at them,' guffawed his father, splutterin Madeira cake across the table. His mother continued, whil the dog crept under the table to devour the falling crumbs.

Paul glanced at the clock – ten past six. His father aros to answer the phone. Taking advantage of his disappearanc Paul asked to be excused, standing on the dog's tail in th process. Just at that moment his sister entered, the do stopped yelling, and in the minor confusion Paul crept ou of the back door, away from the awful thought of washin up. Not that his mother would have allowed it, anyway – h always broke a dish.

He quickly made his way to the footbridge. From i lofty steps spotters surveyed four running lines, bot fast and slow. To the south you could see Mossley Hi station with its signal box and goods yard, together wit the tall Home signals controlling all Liverpool-boun traffic. Looking north, you surveyed the rising gradient to Wavertree, presenting an uninterrupted view of approaching trains for approximately half a mile.

Philip had yet to arrive. Tubby Hughes was there, together with classmates Billy ('Badger') Kerr and John Pearson.

'What's been through?' Paul asked the group.

'*Lord Rathmore* on the 4.17,' smirked Tubby. 'I copped her.'

'She was through about a month ago – I saw her on the Two line peg.'

Paul's statement was interrupted by a cry from Pearson, who had spotted that the Down Fast signal was pulled off. En bloc they took up viewing positions on the footbridge steps in eager anticipation, ears straining for the sound of the approaching train. They could hear her now, a distant rumble, rolling towards them with a rhythmic bark. Suddenly she burst into view, amid a cloud of steam and smoke, her regulator fully open as she approached their position.

'"Jube"!' cried Paul, noticing the lubricators flanking the smokebox.

'It's a special!' shouted Tubby.

'Four fifty-five ninety-six!' screamed Paul above the roar, her number visible. The engine charged towards them, all heads turning in unison as she tore past, the clicking of her nine carriages echoing in the still evening air. Quickly she disappeared from view, leaving a smoking wake, and silence returned.

'*Bahamas**, ruddy stink!' blurted Paul. They were all disappointed.

'She was on the Newcastle last week – I saw her in Lime Street,' voiced John Pearson, 'She could do with a clean.'

Bahamas was an Edge Hill-based engine, and no stranger to the line. She represented a class of 190 express passenger engines built by the LMS during the 1930s, a popular class with the spotters as they all bore names. Collectively they were known as the 'Jubilee' Class, although Edge Hill drivers

'Jubilee' No 45596 *Bahamas* was another disappointing 'stink', but wa
lucky enough to be saved for preservation. On 2 April 1966, still at worl
she is seen on an SLS special at Wigan. *John Corkill*

called them '5XPs'.

'How many namers have you got now, Tubby?'

'What, "Jubs", Paul? Oh, about 45.'

'No, all namers!' shouted Paul. 'As a matter of fact, I'm thinking of going to Crewe on Saturday. Who's coming?'

'I'm game,' said Tubby.

John Pearson shrugged. 'I can't – I'd like to, but I've got to go to town with my Mum.'

'Mummy's boy,' grinned Tubby, enjoying the pleasure of the pointed remark – he was well used to them himself.

'Oh shut up, fatty! Anyway, you're just a beginner. I've got over 200 namers,' came the angry retort.

'Smoke on the Up Slow.' Badger's eyes were ever sharp. All arguments were forgotten as they all stared anxiously in the direction of the smoke.

'"Coffee Pot"!' they chorused. They had sighted a neglected member of the London & North Western Railway's 'G2' goods class. Unpopular with crews, due to their uncomfortable cabs and dubious braking system, they were powerful engines, performing much useful work. Bellowing smoke abundantly, she increased speed on the falling incline, the snap of couplings increasing with her change of pace. Her train was not particularly long, approximately twenty wagons, but she made a handsome sight with steam escaping from various openings in her frame.

'She's on a trip to Speke Sidings. I bet she won't travel so swiftly up the gradient on her return. You'd think they would clean them a bit more often.' Tubby was shouting, to make him-self heard. 'Four ninety-four thirty-seven.'

Most of the Liverpool-based 'Super Ds', or 'Coffee Pots' as they were known locally, were based at Edge Hill. Rocking gently, she passed the footbridge before disappearing in a cloud of smoke and steam.

Another locomotive tore unexpectedly out of the fading haze. '"Scot"! "Scot"!' went up the excited cry. Taken by surprise, they now found themselves staring at a 'Royal Scot' Class locomotive roaring towards them on a Liverpool-

At Ditton Junction in 1960, looking up the bank towards Runcorn, an unidentified 'Super D' heads a lengthy Northwich to St Helens Clock Face goods. The train has left the fast line and is about to enter Ditton yard, where the engine will run round the train before proceeding tender-first up the slow line to St Helens. Another 'Super D' rests in sidings performing the '99 shunt', nicknamed the 'Widnes Warrior' duty by local BR employees. *Brian Cassidy*

'Coffee Pots' in store at Bletchley shed in July 1962. They were powerful engines, but unpopular with crews. *Ray Ruffell, Silver Link Publishing collection*

bound express. Transfixed, they watched her approach, her wheels racing in a flurry of power as she attacked the bank, steaming arrogantly past their position amid a chorus of boos. No 46124, *London Scottish*! Moans of derision, and disappointment. Another Edge Hill engine, and a 'stink'!

Events continued in a like manner. A couple of 'Black Fives' made appearances, together with another 'Jubilee' on a fitted freight. Unfortunately, she too had been seen previously, increasing their frustration, and prompting Tubby and Pearson to snipe at each other at every opportunity.

Philip had now arrived, much to Paul's relief. Paul wanted to know if his pal was game for his proposed trip – up to now Tubby would be his sole companion. 'Fancy a trip to Crewe on Saturday, Phil?'

he boys saw 'Royal Scot' No 46124 *London Scottish* roaring past on a verpool-bound express. Here sister loco No 46112 *Sherwood Forester* shes through Bletchley on 30 April 1960 with a special heading for Vembley for a schoolboys' international match. *Frank Hornby*

25

'What time you going?'

'Oh, a little after seven. Tubby's going. Come on, it should be a good day.'

'I've got my paper round to do – you'll have to make it later.'

'Well, all right, what about eight? We could catch the "Shamrock Express" from Mossley Hill.'

'I think my Dad may be driving the "Shamrock" on Saturday. I'm not sure though – I'll have to check.'

Paul smiled excitedly. Visions of a cab trip to Crewe formed in his mind. Looking at Tubby, his visions faded. With a sigh he called Tubby over. 'Tubby, we're going at eight now.' He simply nodded. 'We'll all meet outside Mossley Hill Station at 7.50.' Paul had already taken charge.

'What do you think we'll see at Crewe, Phil?' asked Paul tentatively.

'Oh, the usual – "Semis", "Patriots", "Scots", "Jubs" and the odd "Brit". With a bit of luck we may see some new diesels.'

'Ugh!' grimaced Paul, pulling a face.

Ignoring the gesture, Philip enquired, 'Did you see *Railway Roundabout* on TV the other night?'

'Yes, good, wasn't it? What did you think of the preserved Midland Compound?'

Their conversation was broken by the sound of a furious argument. Tubby and Pearson were at it again and deciding that there was only one way to settle the issue, they approached Philip.

Tubby pointed accusingly at Pearson. 'He says he's seen a "Streak" at Carlisle.'

'I did!' screamed Pearson. 'I saw it last year when I was on my way to my Gran's.'

'You're a liar!' retorted Tubby. 'You don't get "Streaks" at Carlisle, do you, Phil?'

Philip shuffled uneasily before replying. 'Well, you do occasionally get them at Carlisle Canal shed.'

'There!' interrupted Pearson. 'Told you so – I'm not

'You don't get "Streaks" at Carlisle, do you, Phil?' Here's one - No 60009 *Union of South Africa* on a southbound working on 22 April 1962! *Ron Herbert*

ar, you know,' and he walked off, leaving Tubby slightly emused.

'I was going to add that I've never seen one there,' said Philip. 'Still, he's probably telling the truth.'

'For a change…' muttered an aggrieved Tubby.

The sight of a light engine travelling on the Up Slow reated a flurry of excitement.

'"Blink Niner"'! went up the cry. Paul fumbled for his ABC loco book – her number, 92015, shone like a beacon. Reaching the desired page, he glanced eagerly at the list of umbers, letting out a whoop of joy. A cop, at last – things vere looking up! These engines seldom made sojourns to his stretch of line.

It had now gone 8.00pm, resulting in the anticipated rrival of the Liverpool-bound 'Shamrock Express', which timulated the adrenalin. Three other trainspotters had uietly arrived on the bridge, two being complete strangers. adger, answering a call of nature, had urinated in a dark

'Blink Niner' 9F 2-10-0 No 92203 — later preserved — is seen on a[n] express passenger working at Exeter St David's during the 1950s. She wa[s] photographed by one of the author's old school pals during his summe[r] holiday in sunny Devon. She has probably arrived from the North o[f] England, as she carries LM Region reporting stickers, her smokebo[x] number clearly visible. *Author's collection*

Another 9F, this one photographed at Reading (Southern) shed on 31 Ju[ne] 1963. These engines proved popular on heavy summer schedules, whe[n] their power and speed could be put to good use. *Ray Ruffell, Silver Li[nk] Publishing collection*

corner, only to be disturbed by the new arrivals. Pearson was supposed to have been keeping watch.

'It might have been a woman!' Badger exclaimed, looking distinctly embarrassed.

All eyes were focussed on the Down Fast signal. If Philip knew what was hauling the 'Shamrock', he kept it to himself. No one had a collection like Philip's. He had seen every 'Coronation', 'Patriot', 'Princess' and 'Scot'. Only a few Scottish-based 'Jubilees' and 'Class Fives' would prove to be of interest, and he was unlikely to see them tonight.

'Two line peg.' It was the express. Ears strained.

'She's coming!' someone cried. A distant whistle wailed, followed by a growing roar.

'It's a "Scot"!' shouted Paul, focussing on the approaching express. The engine raced towards them, her red buffers gleaming in the evening sunlight, her exhaust resonant, screaming in unleashed venom. Unexpectedly her whistle sounded again, and the driver waved briefly, acknowledging their presence. Seconds later she was storming up the gradient, making light of her heavy fifteen-coach express. No 45525 *Colwyn Bay*. Yet another 'stink'! It really wasn't their night.

The locomotive in charge had been a rebuilt 'Patriot', which were similar in appearance to the rebuilt 'Royal Scot' Class, resulting in Paul's mistake. The un-rebuilt 'Patriots', or 'Baby Scots' as they were popularly known, resembled the original 'Royal Scots' introduced by the LMS in 1927.

Paul had seen enough. 'I'm going,' he told Philip. 'See you tomorrow in class.'

'Aren't you waiting for the "Merseyside Express"?'

'No, I'm off – don't forget Saturday.'

As Paul said farewell to his chums his mind was already at Crewe. Would Saturday ever come?

2
CREWE

The hostile face behind the window looked like a circular cheese. 'How old are you? Come off it, you're at least fifteen.'

'No I'm not,' Paul exhorted in a tense tone.

The clerk called over the Station Master and the pair gave him a long look. Paul was getting exasperated.

'Half Special Cheap Day Return to Crewe please,' he repeated, looking at his pals for support. The time was a little after 8.00am and he was late. Tubby and Philip already had their tickets – now he was suffering from the effects of his height. He pointed to his school badge, whereupon the clerk reluctantly gave him his requested ticket after a brief nod from the Station Master. Paul picked it up and breathed a sigh of relief.

'Thank goodness for that!' he exclaimed with a feeling of euphoria. 'Is your Dad driving the "Shamrock", Phil?'

'No, he's on the Birmingham. We'll probably see him at Crewe later – I've told him to watch out for us.'

Chattering continuously, they left the booking hall and proceeded to Platform 1 via the enclosed ramp. Walking down the long dim tunnel was quite an experience, its uneven wooden floor a trap for the unwary. One couldn't help feeling nostalgic about the old Mossley Hill station, Paul thought – typical London & North Western in design, a solid structure that had survived two World Wars. There was something about the place – perhaps it was the atmosphere. Coal fires burned in the waiting rooms, brasses gleamed, and flowers bloomed in wooden tubs, all contributing to create a feeling of warmth and welcome. Little did he know that within a year it would all be gone, demolished in the name of progress.

This is Mossley Hill station in the late 1950s, the starting point for many of Paul's adventures. A typical solidly built LNWR structure, it had survived two World Wars. Photographed from Platform 2, the view is looking up the gradient towards Wavertree and Edge Hill, and the footbridge featured in the previous chapter can be glimpsed in the distance, spanning the four running lines. The up 'Shamrock' and down 'Merseyside' expresses stopped here prior to electrification. *Courtesy of Irwell Press Ltd*

D215 tooted briefly as she drew away from the station, caring little for the curses drifting from the middle carriage. Paul was disappointed to say the least. 'Just our flaming luck, a ruddy diesel!' He couldn't believe it. Philip, on the other hand, was quite pleased with their charge – now he could compare performances. Tubby said little, being preoccupied with his bar of chocolate. Philip positioned himself by a convenient window. Paul should have realised that the chances of diesel traction were high. He glanced at his pal, sharing a joke with Tubby – clearly his mood wa[s] over.

Crewe finally arrived after an uneventful journey. Spek[e] shed had produced a silent line of withdrawn 'Coffee Pot[s]' and very little else. The diesel proved to be no faster tha[n] steam, so Paul was wearing his 'I told you so' expressio[n], much to Philip's disgust. Edge Hill-based 'Princess' 'Pacifi[c]' No 46203 *Princess Margaret Rose** snorted past their trai[n] just outside the station. Of lengthy proportions, these wer[e] elegant and powerful locomotives, frequently handling th[e] prestige intercity workings. She was, however, a 'stink'!

Five minutes later found them mixing with other spotter[s] and sampling the gossip. What had they missed, the[y] enquired – apparently not very much. There was a Grea[t] Western 'Hall' in Crewe South shed, and rumours of a 'Cla[n]' in Crewe North – unfortunately no one had seen her, at lea[st] not yet.

Tubby had an idea. 'Listen, why don't we have somethin[g] to eat – I'm starving!'

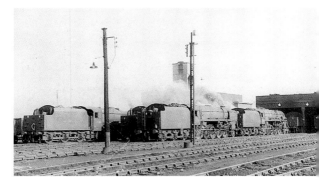

Speke Junction shed late in life in February 1967, with 8F 2-8-0 No 4813[?] and 9F 2-10-0s Nos 92050 and 92022 visible. *The late J. M. Tolson, courte[sy] of Frank Hornby*

dge Hill-based 'Princess' 'Pacific' No 46203 *Princess Margaret Rose* went n to have an eventful career. Withdrawn in 1962, she was bought by utlins and, after cosmetic restoration at Crewe, was displayed at the wllheli holiday camp, as seen here in July 1966. In 1975 she moved to the 1idland Railway Centre at Butterley. Butlins sold the locomotive in 1985, nd she was restored to full working order in 1990. *Ray Ruffell, Silver Link* ublishing collection

Paul gasped. 'Blimey, Tubby, you've just devoured a bar f chocolate – have an apple for now and we'll all eat later.' ubby grimaced.

'He's a gannet,' whispered Philip, Tubby having decided o visit the loo. 'I bet the sly fox is going for a quick nibble.'

'There's a Great Western "Hall" in Crewe South shed' was the news that greeted Paul and his friends. This is No 6958 *Oxburgh Hall* at Crewe South on 30 October 1960. *John Corkill*

Tubby suddenly reappeared in an excitable state clutching a sandwich, '"Brit"!' he screamed. 'There's "Brit" coming up the opposite platform – come on or we' miss her!'

Soon he was to realise the inaccuracy of his statemen – this engine was unique. No 71000 *Duke of Gloucester* shimmered under a weakening sun, the locomotive's massiv proportions outstanding – a magnificent and powerfu machine. For a second she was lost in a haze of steam a she halted at signals at the end of the platform. Paul mad a dash for her, hearing the clatter of footsteps in his wake Soon he was alongside the engine, her gleaming paintwor suggesting recent toil. He was swiftly joined by a breathles Tubby. Philip, deciding to stroll, was lost amid a swarm c spotters who rapidly besieged the locomotive. Paul gazed i awe at her Caprotti valve gear, cylinders and motion, ever part seemingly covered in a film of oil, echoing competenc and sound design. Philip eventually arrived and nodde towards the engine.

'Well, Tubby, she might resemble a "Brit", but there th similarity ends.'

'Why?' Tubby asked, red-faced.

'My Dad doesn't care for her. He says she's a poo steamer.'

Outwardly similar to 'Britannia' 'Pacific', th solitary 8P 4-6-2 N 71000 *Duke of Glouceste* was something of disappointment in servic and is seen here arrivir at Wolverton on an u stopping train on 25 Ju 1962. Modified whe preserved, she is now very successful machin *Ray Ruffell, Silver Lir Publishing collection*

Paul climbed onto the footplate steps and stared into the cab at the array of gauges. Within seconds his gaze was returned by the locomotive's smiling driver, a man in his late fifties with twinkling eyes and weathered features.

'Nosey aren't you? Want to take a proper look?' he asked, winking at Paul.

'Do I?' He was up on the footplate in a flash. He felt suddenly guilty. 'What about my mates?' Tubby was, however, already behind him.

'One at a time!' shouted the driver, halting his pal on the footplate steps. 'I don't want a tribe up here.'

It was a roomy cab and Paul stared towards the gauges again, trying to puzzle out their function. His eyes fell on the speedometer – this gauge he understood. 'Do you often get up to 90 miles an hour?' he asked curiously.

'Now and again – depends on the wind.' The fireman had taken it upon himself to answer the question, bringing a chuckle from the driver.

'Is she a poor steamer? My pal says she is.' Paul felt as if he was checking up on Philip.

'Oh, an expert is he?' beamed the driver. 'Well she's a beggar at times, and will keep Joe busy,' motioning towards the fireman. 'But she'll get us to Carlisle, I dare say.'

The driver now gestured for Tubby to come aboard, politely asking a reluctant Paul to step down. Descending the cab steps he felt suddenly cold. My, it had been warm in there. Philip looked bored.

'Why don't you have a look?'

'No thanks, I've been on her before in Crewe North shed.' He was about to continue when a long blast of the whistle signified her departure.

Tubby tumbled down the cab steps. 'She's off!' he uttered excitedly.

'Get away!' wisecracked Paul.

A glistening face loomed above them. 'Bye, lads!' The fireman smiled briefly then returned his gaze to the track ahead. With a mighty hiss she moved forward, her exhaust increasing with the quickening of her motion, all eyes feastin on this portrait of energy. She was destined to take over Scottish express, which had previously arrived from Londo behind Nos 45446 and 44871*, two perspiring 'Black Fives Once uncoupled, the pair preceded to Crewe North she and, after running forward, *Duke of Gloucester* reverse on to her designated train. Masses of spotters immediatel raced to watch her couple up, including our trio, who wer temporally distracted by the arrival of 'Jubilee' *Zanzibar*.

Watching the 'Pacific' couple up proved to be an anti climax. The driver had not acknowledged them, as he wa preoccupied with his charge, and Paul felt a twinge c disappointment at this lack of recognition. With a frightenin roar the safety valves opened, prompting many onlookers t retreat. Doggedly, Paul, Tubby and Philip stayed to watch th train's imminent departure. Within seconds whistles blev doors slammed and, after a short blast on her chime whistle the 'Pacific' moved forward, her wheels slipping violentl

'Jubilee' 4-6-0 No 45638 *Zanzibar* was photographed on a decided mixed parcels train at Wembley on 18 August 1962. *Frank Hornby*

efore finding adhesion. Suddenly the safety valves cut out
nd gingerly she began to claw her way out of the station,
ne noise deafening as her chimney belched out a column of
nick black smoke. Paul counted fourteen laden carriages –
uite a load, he mused, as he watched the train thread its
ray through the maze of points and crossings north of the
tation. They watched her disappear, a mournful blast from
er whistle bidding a final farewell to all admirers.

'Bet she gets a pilot at Preston,' chuckled Philip.

'I bet she doesn't,' snapped Paul, defending the engine
nd wishing he was still in her cab.

Unknown to our trio, *Duke of Gloucester* would make it
 Carlisle unassisted, even if somewhat belatedly.

This modern 'Pacific' had been introduced in 1954,
nd was to remain the sole member of her class, an engine
esigned to haul some of the heaviest and fastest expresses
 Great Britain. She was built at Crewe and was based
ere for most of her working life. History was not kind
 this locomotive – her success was not outstanding, but
ne presented a superb spectacle when in steam. As with
nost of the British Railways-built locomotives, her working
fe was short, being withdrawn in December 1962. After
nguishing in Barry scrapyard, South Wales, she was moved,
iinus cylinders and valve gear, to the Great Central Railway
eritage line in April 1974 for restoration. The rest, as they
ay, is history. Today she can be seen performing on steam
ecials throughout the UK – an astounding achievement,
flecting the professionalism and tenacity of the restoration
am involved.

The threat presented by diesels had become a harsh
ality by the autumn of 1959, D215 having borne this out.
heir infiltration into former steam workings was gaining
nomentum; English Electric Type 4s formed the nucleus
f the attack, and Paul was increasingly sickened by the
rowing numbers of these dreaded machines. Philip, on the
ther hand, was philosophical about the newcomers. From
 collector's point of view they were most welcome, being

quickly entered in his *ABC Combined Volume*. The fact tha
they were replacing steam didn't bother him unduly; afte
all, there were enough steam engines around to satisfy mos
steam fanatics. As if on cue, English Electric Type 4 D21
purred through.

'What does your Dad think of diesels, Phil?' Tubb
muttered the question as if dreading the reply.

'Well,' Philip took a deep breath, 'he says there's n
challenge with a diesel, not like driving steam. If he had hi
way he'd continue to work on both. Since they introduce
diesels at Edge Hill a couple of drivers have suffered hear

In 1952 former LMS main-line diesel No 10001 trundles through Spel
with the up 'Shamrock' express, having stopped at Mossley Hill static
en route. It would be another seven years before main-line diesels,
the shape of English Electric Type 4s, made inroads into intercity steal
workings, dismaying Paul and many local spotters. *Brian Cassidy*

attacks, probably through lack of exercise, and that worrie
him. Still, he says diesels are here to stay.'

Paul was hoping Philip would say something bad abou
them, but he didn't; now he was expounding the merits o

During the early 1960s some of the initial batch of Type 4 English Electric diesels operating on the London Midland Region were named after well-known liners, thus it was possible to record a name belonging to one of the usurpers of steam. In this photograph taken at Wolverhampton Low Level in 1963, No 7014 *Caerhays Castle* is waiting to take over from No D217 *Corinthia*, which has arrived from the north via Crewe and Shrewsbury with a heavy express for the South of England. Although powerful, the Type 4s were extremely heavy, and the modified 'Castle' would probably prove to be the speedier. *John Burnett*

the newly introduced 'Peak' Class – it really was too much. Paul's rising anger overflowed. 'Well, you can keep your ruddy diesels, and electrics for that matter – give a steam engine a clear road and she'll fly!' His voice faltered. Coming up the platform was a gleaming crimson-liveried Stanier 'Duchess' 'Pacific'. He stood mesmerised – not more than 20 feet away stood one of the most powerful express passenger locomotives in Great Britain. '"Semi"!' he screamed, straining his vocal cords to the limit.

Cheering drifted towards them from other spotters who were now running alongside the engine. Paul raced towards

her, trailed by a lumbering Tubby. What was her number
Ah, it appeared at last through the swirling steam – 4622
*Duchess of Hamilton**.

'Cop, cop!' went up the joyous cry. Paul literally dance
with jubilation. Tubby also beamed. Philip, however, looke
unimpressed.

'Pity you've seen all the "Semis", Phil,' said Paul.

'Oh I still get a thrill out of seeing them, Paul – she's a
good cop.' He smiled weakly and sounded unconvincing.

The trio walked alongside the locomotive, eyeing ever
detail of her motion, Philip eager to answer any question
about her performance or any other technical query. To
their surprise, the engine uncoupled and, after a brief toot
clanked off to the sheds. They waited intently – what would

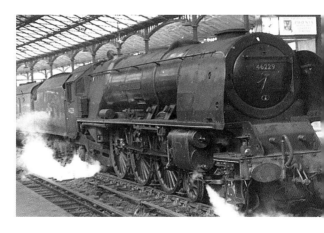

No 46229 *Duchess of Hamilton* was a notable cop for Paul at Crewe. She i
seen here at Euston in about 1961, and following withdrawal in 1964 wa
another Butlins purchase, being displayed at that company's Minehea
holiday camp. In 1975 she was placed on indefinite loan to the Nationa
Railway Museum at York. *Frank Hornby*

replace her? The answer was quickly provided. Reversing on to the train was another 'Duchess', only this time she was green. Tension mounted.

'Oh no, not 46249 *City of Sheffield*!' Groans of derision went up from most onlookers.

'Well, you can't be lucky all the time,' said Philip. Tubby wasn't listening; he just smiled, having just increased his collection.

'Haven't you seen her before, Tubby?' asked an astonished Paul. 'She's been at Edge Hill more times than I've had hot dinners.' Obviously he hadn't.

After watching the re-coupling operation they sat down on a platform trolley to watch the 'Duchess' depart. 'Patriot' No 45527 *Southport* stole through on a southbound express, quickly followed by No 46141 *The North Staffordshire Regiment*, a popular member of the 'Royal Scot' Class

'Duchess' 'Pacific' No 46249 *City of Sheffield* was an Edge Hill regular, and is seen here at Lancaster on 5 May 1962. Among the remarks scrawled on her tender is 'Scrap the diesels'! *Ron Herbert*

judging by her reception.

Fowler Class 4 tank No 42375 coasted to a halt on her way to the sheds just as Tubby opened his bag. 'I'm having something to eat,' he declared. 'I'm starving.'

Paul was tempted to say 'Not again', but thought better of it – after all, why not? He too opened his bag and soon they were all eating.

'What's in your sandwiches, Phil?' asked Tubby.

'I've got Sandwich Spread.'

'Mine's luncheon meat,' exclaimed Tubby. 'I'll swap you some.'

The friends saw 'Patriot' No 45527 *Southport* at Crewe on a southbound express. She is seen here in fine condition at Longsight shed, Manchester on 18 September 1960. *The late W. G. Boyden, courtesy of Frank Hornby*

'How about two cheese for a couple of yours, Tubby?' Paul removed the requested amount and replaced them with his own, staring at the 'Duchess' that was about to depart. Effortlessly she moved forward, an engine of supreme appearance making light of her twelve-coach Scottish express. They were still eating when she faded from view.

Paul looked towards Crewe Works, wondering what

The 'Jubilee' was quickly followed by No 46141 *The North Staffordshire Regiment*, a popular member of the 'Royal Scot' Class judging from her reception by the spotters at Crewe. This portrait was taken at Carlisle Upperby shed on 11 June 1964. *Frank Hornby*

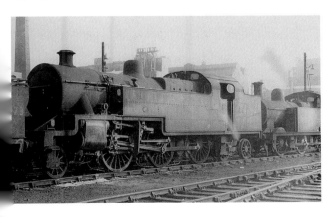

Fowler Class 4 tank No 42375 was another loco spotted at Crewe. She is seen here after withdrawal at Derby Works on 25 February 1962. *The late J. M. Tolson, courtesy of Frank Hornby*

surprises lay less than a mile away. It might have been a million miles – there was no chance of gaining entry without a pass. Even though production had ceased, Crewe Works still overhauled steam engines, and they would on memorable occasions emerge freshly painted. On his previous visit, Paul had seen an ex-works 'Coffee Pot' and she'd looked wonderful, but this day would prove disappointing.

'I wonder what's in the works?' voiced Paul wistfully.

'Probably some "Semis", "Standards", "Jubs", "Scots", Stanier 8Fs, "Blink Niners" and "Mickeys". You're never quite sure what you'll find until you enter.'

Philip had explored the works several times with his father and spoke from experience. 'Do you know there are a couple of former Caledonian Railway "Pugs" in there? Came as quite a surprise, I can tell you. They were shunting in the works.'

'Wish I could see them,' said Tubby between bananas.

'Me too,' interrupted Paul, looking towards the works.

'Tell you what – next time I go with my Dad, I'll ask if you can come.'

'Would you?' They both flushed with excitement.

For the next few minutes Philip was plied with questions. Did he think his Dad would agree? Why not ask him when he arrived later? How many engines would be in the works? And so on. Philip was highly relieved when a 'Britannia' 'Pacific' materialised hauling the up 'Irish Mail'. Tubby and Paul raced off to meet her, leaving him somewhat anxious. Within an hour his father would be arriving, then what? They might be disappointed. He cursed under his breath – he should never have opened his mouth.

No 70045 *Lord Rowallan* received a mixed reception, cheers and boos clashing with the sound of escaping steam. One ungentlemanly spotter made a rude gesture at the locomotive, only to have it returned in similar fashion by her leering fireman, amusing all except a station inspector.

The 'Britannia' 'Pacifics' were outstanding performers when expertly handled, some lasting until the final days of team. No 70045 was one of five allocated to Crewe North, or hauling the heavy 'Irish Mail' trains. The entire class was tted with chime whistles, making them easily identifiable.

Four hours later found the trio back on the platform trolley lancing through their spotting books. It had been a hectic

Britannia' No 70045 *Lord Rowallan* received a mixed reception from the ssembled spotters at Crewe station. This photograph shows the 'Pacific' ear Lancaster. *Ron Herbert*

eriod, Paul reflected. Why Philip hadn't been disappointed hen his father failed to arrive on the Birmingham remained mystery. Due to heavy absenteeism at Edge Hill shed, rivers had been substituted; the replacement driver had vited them on to the footplate before relating the tale to hilip. Rather surprisingly, the express had been in charge f 'Crab' 2-6-0 No 42849. When questioned, the driver dmitted that this was due to his allocated engine, 'Patriot' *Caernarvon*, failing on shed, leaving him little choice but to ake the spare. Little time had been lost, giving him some atisfaction. When Philip asked the driver what he thought of the 'Crab', he had simply replied, 'Rough!'

Paul awoke from his stupor to find his pals holding a quiet tête-à-tête with another spotter. However, the fascinating sight sneaking up on them quickly halted all further conversation. Ivatt Class 2 tank No 41229 coupled to 'Jinty' No 47516, both of which were in steam, clanked and groaned along pulling a brace of 'Coffee Pots' and No 45689 *Ajax*, a grubby 'Jubilee'. Hastily all numbers were written down as an attentive audience watched the procession make its way painfully to the sheds. Suddenly No

'Crab' 2-6-0 No 42849 arrived on an express, substituting for a failed 'Patriot'. When Philip asked the driver what he thought of the 2-6-0, he replied, 'Rough!' Receiving their nickname from their unusual high-set angled cylinders, sister loco No 42809 is seen at Ayr shed on 7 June 1963 awaiting the cutter's torch. *Ray Ruffell, Silver Link Publishing collection*

6211 *Queen Maud* swaggered through with a fifteen-coach Liverpool express.

'Getting busy again, isn't it?' yelled Tubby. Emphasising the point, 'Royal Scot' Class No 46159 *The Royal Air Force* put in an appearance on a Manchester train.

'Blimey, it's Joe's engine!' blurted Paul, much to their amusement.

The arrival of No 45530 *Sir Frank Ree* in tandem with No 45514 *Holyhead* caused a major sensation. Double-headers were not entirely rare, but two rebuilt 'Patriots', that was different.

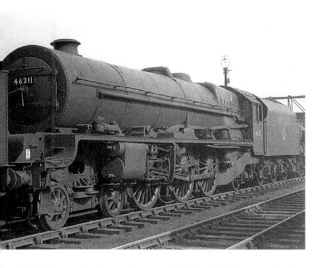

No 46211 *Queen Maud*, seen here on 23 March 1962, was the first 'Princess' 'Pacific' to be cut up. *John Corkill*

Philip, meanwhile, had other things on his mind and called out accordingly, 'There's a sight you don't see too

often,' pointing to an old ex-Lancashire & Yorkshire good[...]
engine slowly coming into view from the direction of th[...]
works. '52312!' he cried.

'Wow, look at her open cab – I pity anyone who has t[...]
work in her during a snowstorm,' said Tubby.

Philip promptly took the stage. 'Don't worry, they car[...]
a tarpaulin in case of inclement weather – see, it's rolled u[...]
behind the cab. Makes you realise, though, what those ear[...]
drivers had to face. Just think, in the 1830s all crews we[...]
out in the open, devoid of any form of protection.' Phil[...]

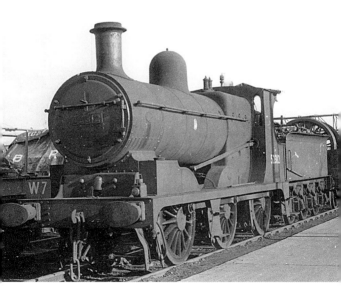

'I bet she's nearly sixty years old – I hope I live that long,' exclaimed Phil[...]
when he saw ex-L&YR 0-6-0 No 52312. The open-cabbed veteran is se[...]
here as the Crewe Works shunter on 6 November 1961. *John Corkill*

was clearly enjoying himself and continued, 'Did you know that for some years drivers had to crawl along the footplate keeping tight hold of the boiler, and oil the various parts while the engine was still in motion?'

'Risky,' gasped Tubby, unwrapping a toffee.

'Some idiots even fastened down their safety valves to gain more speed – no wonder there were accidents,' continued Philip.

Paul couldn't resist butting in. 'Funny you should say that, Phil. I heard that your Dad does that when he's late with the London.'

Tubby spluttered and lost his toffee, while Philip smiled, then nodded towards the old goods engine, now stationary at signals. 'I bet she's nearly sixty years old – I hope I live that long.'

'You will,' chirped Tubby. 'Only the good die young.'

Later three tired locospotters left the Liverpool-bound local at Mossley Hill station. '5.55 – dead on time. I said we'd have a good run behind the "Mogul",' said Paul. All eyes turned towards No 42968*, a small yet powerful locomotive heading their train. True, she had performed well, but with only six coaches her task had been easy.

The group split up at the top of the ramp, arranging to meet after tea at the footbridge. 'By the way, Phil, don't forget to ask your Dad about Crewe Works,' added Paul.

'Me too!' voiced Tubby.

Philip half smiled – how could he forget?.

Soon Paul was home, and on entering he greeted his father, who was earnestly rechecking his football coupon. 'Well, son, how did it go today?'

'Oh, great, Dad – we saw "Semis", "Princesses", "Scots", "Jubilees", "Patriots", "Coffee Pots", Stanier 5s, "WDs", Ivatt and Fowler tanks, "Jinties", "Mickeys", "Moguls", "Standards", "Brits" – oh, and an ex-Lancashire & Yorkshire goods engine.'

His father grunted. 'Is that all?' He was sorry he'd asked.

The Stanier 5MT 2-6-0s were small yet powerful locomotives, and th
friends travelled behind No 42968, one that was later preserved. Her
sister loco No 42954 starts away northwards from Stafford on 19 Augu
1963. *Ray Ruffell, Silver Link Publishing collection*

3
SHED BUNKING

Paul's eyes flickered momentarily from his homework to the television set, then returned to his chemistry book. Seconds later they returned to the television. He loathed chemistry, and *William Tell* was much more interesting.

'Paul, go upstairs and do your homework – no sense in you doing it down here.' Mrs Carr's eyes rested on her inattentive son as Mr Carr grunted his approval.

'But Mum, Joan's got her gramophone on in the bedroom it will be too noisy.'

She wavered. 'Well, do one or the other, either watch the television or do your homework, not both.'

'Yes, Mum.'

His chemistry book was discarded – time for that later. Or was there? The 'Shamrock Express' was on his itinerary for the evening – perhaps he would also wait for the 'Merseyside Express'. An Austrian fell dead, then another. Yes, he would wait for the 'Merseyside Express', just to see 'Princess Royal' 'Pacific'.

By the time William Tell had driven off several more Austrians, Paul had decided to cycle to Speke shed, motivated by the sight of the expresses rounding the curve south of Allerton station. The trains fairly heeled over at this point, and the footbridge at the commencement of this section provided a wonderful platform for observing the spectacle. Equally, it served as a vantage point for spotting all locomotives using the shed, not to mention the Cheshire Lines traffic. Of course he would ask Philip and Tubby to accompany him. With a satisfied sigh he tapped his chemistry book – that could wait until tomorrow.

Tubby was as usual lagging behind, as Philip surged

Chester (Midland)-based BR Standard Class 4 4-6-0 No 75013 leans into the curve at Speke as she accelerates away from Allerton station with a Chester train. The trains fairly heeled over at this point, and the footbridge at the commencement of the section provided a wonderful platform for observing this spectacle; equally it served as a vantage point for spotting all engines using the shed, and the Cheshire Lines. *The late Jim Peden.*

On 10 April 1958, minutes after passing Speke Junction shed, former LMS 4F No 44352 steams out of the morning mist near Woodside signal box with an unfitted goods; the sidings on the left served a local coal merchant. This evocative study features a less than glamorous workhorse whose number would nevertheless be swiftly entered into your *ABC*. *The late Jim Peden*

ahead against an increasing wind. Funny how the wind appeared to be always against them when they were in a hurry, Paul mused. He bit his lip and pressed harder on the pedals.

'Come on, Tubby – get a move on or we'll be late.'

His words carried on the wind, but if Tubby had heard his pal's urgent cry, the effort required was unforthcoming. A heavy shower engulfed them; 20 seconds later it ceased, leaving them bedraggled.

'I'm soaked,' panted Tubby.

'Me too,' complained Paul, glancing at the evening sky. 'No sign of any more rain. Anyway, we're nearly there.'

'Liar,' whispered Tubby, exchanging glances with Philip. They continued, but Tubby lagged even further behind, bringing exasperated groans from his pals. Doubling back, Paul pulled up alongside his labouring pal. 'Here, Tubby, swap bikes.' His wet companion immediately brightened, Paul's racer providing the necessary stimulus. Ten minutes later Tubby was asking Paul to catch up, leering as he did so. Paul silently cursed Tubby and his cycle, grudgingly conceding that it had not been one of his better ideas.

They could smell Speke engine shed long before it came into view. The pungent smell of smoke beckoned on the wind, and the boys cycled madly towards their goal. Under a railway bridge, up a short hill and there she lay, crammed with grimy locomotives, mostly mixed traffic and freight classes, although there were some surprises. What a sight! Enthralled, they gazed along the rows.

'"Jube"!' cried Philip, pointing her out.

'Aye, and a "Blink Niner", plus lots and lots of "Mickeys", 8Fs and "Crabs",' Paul added. 'How much time have we got before the "Shamrock", Phil?'

'About ten minutes – not enough time to bunk around. Let's go to the footbridge and see the "Shamrock". We can come back and explore the shed.'

Twenty minutes passed before the delayed express made an appearance, hauled by No 46106 *Gordon Highlander*, the only member of the 'Royal Scot' Class to carry British Railways-type smoke deflectors. Moans of disappointment were carried on the wind – they had been hoping for something better.

Minutes earlier ex-LNER 'J39' No 64717 had plodded along the former Cheshire Lines route, heading an unfitted goods towards Manchester. The old Great Central route into the city encompassed the former Cheshire Lines system, a path taken by many former LNER express locomotives. The electrification of the former Great Central Woodhead line in the early 1950s had greatly reduced their numbers. Only the odd ex-LNER 'B1', 'O4', 'K3' or 'J39' clung to what had once been familiar ground for 'C1s', 'B17s', 'D10/11s' and 'D9s', which were now just a memory.

Trainspotters considered the Cheshire Lines a boring railway. Ex-LMS Stanier and Fairburn tank engines ruled

Ex-LNER 'J39' No 64717 was seen on the former Cheshire Lines route. The next-numbered member of class, No 64718, stands on the CLC shed at Walton-on-the-Hill, Liverpool, on 13 November 1960. *The late J. N. Tolson, courtesy of Frank Hornby*

supreme on the hourly expresses, but who wanted to see them? It was the namers they were after, and all eyes now focussed on a wheezing 'Jubilee', plodding along the former LNWR main line.

'Four fifty-five fifty-three, *Canada* – ugh!' was the cry as her name became decipherable through the drifting smoke. Tubby leaned further over the parapet, receiving a smutty face for his efforts as the engine's exhaust gusted violently in the flurrying wind. Groaning loudly, the filthy engine laboured under the footbridge, each shriek and groan echoing her poor mechanical condition. It was strange to see a member of the class on an unfitted freight; Philip claimed that she could be en route to Crewe Works for overhaul, bringing cursory nods of approval. With steam escaping from every leaking joint, she struggled by, each wagon jarring and banging as she slowly picked up speed before puffing past a row of withdrawn 'Coffee Pots', or 'Super Ds' as Philip insisted on calling them. Soon a pall of smoke obliterated even the brake-van, and her exhaust gradually faded in the gusting wind. A whistle from the direction of the engine shed broke off all further interest in the departing train. Something was about to move, and they stared anxiously towards the shed.

After what seemed an eternity, a locomotive emerged to turn on the triangle. Little could be seen through the swirling

The boys saw scruffy, wheezing 'Jubilee' No 45553 *Canada* on a freight working. The first of the class, No 45552 *Silver Jubilee* herself, is in equally poor condition working a freight at Hest Bank on 13 July 1964. *Ron Herbert*

smoke, much to their annoyance, the wind still conspiring to thwart any serious attempts to trainspot. Another whistle, then she snorted towards them, bursting out of what, moments earlier, had been an impenetrable smoke screen.

'A "Black Five" – not much to get excited about!' shouted Philip. 'That "Jub's" still in the shed – could be a good one!' Hiss words were lost on his mesmerised pal, Paul's gaze remaining fixed on the approaching locomotive.

'Hasn't that "Mickey" got a nameplate?' he shouted excitedly. With renewed intensity, eyes pierced the bellowing smoke. 'Damn this flaming wind!' he snorted.

Seconds later, another gust brought its reward. 'Paul's right!' exclaimed Tubby. 'It is a named "Mickey"!'

Their footsteps echoed down the stairs. Jostling wildly, they raced towards the approaching engine. Tubby tripped and cursed. His pals raced on, leaving him sprawled in the mud. Tubby could see Paul's fist leap into the air – it must be a cop! Clambering to his feet he ran after them. The shriek from the whistle of the 'Black Five' was deafening as he breathlessly watched her steam by. His eyes sought the engine's number. 45154 *Lanarkshire Yeomanry* – a cop! Wow! The crew shouted a remark, snatched on the wind. Tubby couldn't hear it, but he could see they were laughing at him, and he immediately reddened. Glancing in a pool confirmed his fears. In his euphoria he had forgotten about his muddy encounter, not to mention his sooty face. Gosh, what a sight, my Mum will kill me, a thought that motivated a great deal of frantic activity. Joined by his pals, he desperately sought to rid his blazer of clinging mud. Rubbing it only made it worse, a remark voiced earlier by Paul. A ripple of annoyance was arising deep in his frame – Paul's amusing quips straining his patience. Paul now stated that he thought Tubby looked like a 'Black and White Minstrel' and smirked at his dilemma. An explosion was imminent, and it arrived with a roar.

'Call yourselves friends? You lousy lot, you just left me behind as usual. I'm sick of both of you. My Mum will kill me when she sees me, and you think it's funny!' Tubby

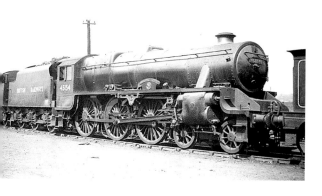

'Black Five' No 45154 *Lanarkshire Yeomanry* – a cop! This was one of the very few 'Black Fives' to carry a name, and this portrait at Perth shed dates from early British Railways days, 18 June 1949. *The late W. G. Boyden, courtesy of Frank Hornby*

...ulped and turned to watch the departing locomotive.

Paul touched his shoulder. 'Sorry, Tubby, we were only ...aving a laugh, weren't we, Phil?' Philip nodded and grinned. ...ome on, we'll bunk around the shed. No sense brushing ...at mud off until it's dried. It will easily brush off, you wait ...d see.'

'That's right,' muttered Philip, having composed himself. ...ubby's sudden eruption had bothered Paul; his pal was ...oted for his placid temperament and he knew he'd gone too ...r. 'Come on, let's go and see what that "Jube" is.' Paul led ...e way, hoping Tubby had not noticed his Mars bar sticking ...t of the mud.

The arrival of 'Britannia' 'Pacific' No 70047 on a fitted ...arcels provided welcome relief, and after five minutes ...l earlier incidents had been completely forgotten. This ...terlude over, they crossed the lines leading to the shed ...fore entering the lines of parked locomotives, eyes alert for authority.

'Did you lock up the bikes, Phil?' asked Tubby, fingerin
a soiled London Midland *ABC*.

'Of course. Hey, where's Paul?'

'Britannia' 'Pacific' No 70047 was the only member of the class to rema
unnamed, and is seen here at the buffer stops at Euston in about 195
Alongside, No 46207 *Princess Arthur of Connaught* has just arrived with th
up 'Merseyside Express'. *A. J. Pike OBE, courtesy of Frank Hornby*

'I'm up here in the "WD".'

'Filthy things, these "Austerities" – pity they never clea
them,' bleated Philip as he followed Tubby up the cab step
Waves of heat engulfed them as they entered the footplat
Paul appeared not to notice their arrival, his concentratio
elsewhere.

'Here, look at these – I mean, look.' Paul held up
magazine containing glossy coloured photographs of sem
naked women. Later he mentally recalled that he had nev
seen Tubby move so quickly.

When Paul entered the cab of a 'WD' in Speke Junction shed he found something he wasn't expecting! This 'Austerity' 2-10-0 was photographed at Motherwell shed on 21 July 1962. *Ron Herbert*

'Cor, let's have a look. Wow, hang on a minute!' Philip held the page as Paul sought to turn to the next. By degrees the magazine unfolded, its audience oblivious to the fact that a rebuilt 'Patriot' had just steamed through.

'I wonder who the book belongs to,' remarked Tubby, looking a little flushed.

'Well, it's mine now,' leered. Paul, about to place it in his back pocket.

'You can't do that Paul, that's stealing,' Tubby huffed.

'Tubby's right. Anyway, it's probably the fireman's,' muttered Philip. 'My Dad says that all they think about is sex.'

Tubby looked perplexed. 'Why, I mean what's so special

about sex?'

A chorus of groans burst from his pals. 'Sometimes, Tubby… Oh, never mind. Come on, let's go.' Paul put down the magazine, and descended the cab steps followed by Philip. Then came Tubby, rather belatedly. Philip checked the shed plate of the 'WD' before proceeding to the next engine. Paul and Tubby never bothered with such trivialities, they just wrote down the numbers of each locomotive before making their way to the next.

They moved on swiftly, writing down an array of numbers, but noting nothing of special interest. 'What a load of rubbish,' came a muted comment. They had now penetrated the interior, and locomotives stood out in the gloom, black silhouettes, refusing to expire. After encountering a couple of drivers, they received an unexpected surprise. Simmering quietly on one of the centre roads was an Ivatt Class 4 tender locomotive, a class rarely seen in Merseyside.

'Blimey, a "Flying Pig"! Where's she from, Phil?' asked Paul.

'Nuneaton.' Her 2B shed plate provided the answer.

'Bit out of her way, isn't she?'

'Well, Paul, they do get around a bit, you know. I bet the fitters love them. Look at all that lovely motion.' Philip went on to explain to an engrossed Tubby the advantages of a high running plate. Paul wrote down her number, 43002, content with his latest cop. The elusive 'Jubilee' was in the next row, and once more adrenalin raced through his veins.

However, groans of displeasure – an Edge Hill 'Jubilee' No 45678 *De Robeck* – what a stink! Seconds later they were on the footplate, examining the controls. Paul sat in the driver's seat as Tubby examined the contents of a white enamelled tea can. 'Looks like dish water – still, it's warm.'

'You're not going to drink some, are you?' Philip gaped.

'Course not – I mean, you don't know where it's been. My Mum told me never to eat or drink left-over food – it's unhygienic.'

'Just as well you're not a driver then. My Dad cooks his

Philip explained the maintenance advantages of the high running plate of the ex-LMS Ivatt 4MT 2-6-0s, nicknamed 'Flying Pigs' from their somewhat unprepossessing appearance. No 43018 stands on Derby shed on 2 October 1966. *Frank Hornby.*

The boys climbed aboard 'Jubilee' No 45678 *De Robeck* at Speke. Here he is passing through Watford Junction on an up special for the Rugby League Cup Final at Wembley on 10 May 1958. *Frank Hornby*

In the summer of 2011 Peter Kelly, former editor of *The Railway Magazine* and *Steam Railway* (left) and the author pose for the camera holding a gleaming replica *De Robeck* nameplate. Not popular with local spotters, the engine was a notorious 'stink'. Based at Edge Hill, she popped up on all sorts of traffic, from express parcels and passenger duties to fitted freights, and was seldom clean! But how the author wishes he could see her now! *Author's collection*

bacon and egg on his shovel,' prattled Philip. 'Bit of coal dust gives it a bit of extra taste – least, that's what my Dad says.'

'Ugh, imagine coal dust in the yolk!' Tubby's face twisted in distain. An amused Paul looked on, trying desperately to add to the proceedings; however, on this occasion he could find nothing to add. Noting that the screw reversing gear was correctly positioned, he gazed wistfully out of the cab window. The seductive warmth of the cab rapidly took effect, and his body soon swayed to an imaginary rhythm. Sixty miles an hour, and a tunnel coming up; unconsciously he reached for the whistle. Shriek…! The muted sudden blast jolted him out of his daydream, and infuriated his pals.

'You great twit!' screamed Philip. 'What did you do that or? Come on, let's go before someone comes.'

They leapt down the steps, then, after glancing around, they sped from the loco, dragging Tubby in the process. Breathlessly they crept around the end of the row.

'You know, Paul, that was really stupid! I mean, why don't you just tell the world that we're here?' puffed Tubby.

Paul retorted angrily, 'Oh, stop worrying, Tubby. Come on – there's no one about. Look, there's that "Blink Niner". Let's go and cab her.'

Leading his pals towards the engine brought an unpleasant surprise. 'You lot! Get out of it! Hop it!' The imposing figure of the shed master had spoken, and their expedition was at an end. Like deflated balloons they returned to their cycles. Paul hardly opened his mouth, having blown it.

'Hey, I copped that "Blink Niner",' chirped Tubby, happier now that their brush with authority was over. No one spoke.

Any of the occupants of the nearby flats could have been excused for showing alarm at the commotion hurtling their way on the near gale-force wind. The tirade, swift, sudden and endless, flowed from Paul, who, on finding his bicycle had a flat tyre, burst forth a torrent of abuse at Tubby. Apart from the humiliation suffered moments earlier, this was the final straw.

Tubby looked aghast. 'Could be a slow puncture,' he muttered without conviction. 'Just as well we've got the wind behind us going home. What about the "Merseyside Express"? Aren't we going to wait for it?'

'No,' came the tart reply. Bending down, Paul quickly released his pump and went to work. They watched as he fingered the tyre – at least it was up for now. 'Come on, let's go.'

On Paul's command they all mounted, Tubby feeling in his pocket for an elusive Mars bar. Pushed by the wind, they made good progress, apart from an impromptu halt, producing more frantic activity.

Mr Carr watched the boys approach, glancing occasionally in their direction between bouts of rose-pruning. 'Peace' looked splendid, as did 'Queen Elizabeth', but this wind could spoil their blooms. The sound of a moving roof tile increased his concern. It looked as if they were in for a real blow. The clatter of the drive gate provided a pleasant diversion. But someone or something had upset his son.

'What's up with you, eh?'

'Got a puncture.'

'Oh, is that all? When I was your age I had more punctures than I care to remember. Cycles were heavier then,' he prattled on, indifferent to Philip's remarks about penny-farthings. Yes, he could remember his bicycle well, hub brakes and all. Suddenly he shot a glance at Paul.

'Did you finish your homework?'

'Not yet,' came the plaintive reply, puzzled by his father's sudden switch of thought.

'Aye, well, make sure you do it before you go to bed.'

Paul smarted, knowing full well his pals had overheard his father's instructions; he would endure some mickey-taking in class tomorrow. Tubby's fumbling and apprehension worried Mr Carr.

'Lost something, son?'

'Oh, only a Mars bar. I could have sworn I had it with me when we started out.' He smiled apologetically, somewhat embarrassed.

'If I were you, I'd go home and change. You look as if you've been fighting.'

They all grinned. 'Course not, Mr Carr,' smirked Philip. 'Anyway, we'd better be going now.'

They mounted, calling Paul over before departure. Tubby whispered, 'Paul, don't forget to do your homework!'

With this gleeful utterance the pair shot off, leaving their speechless pal.

It had not been one of his better nights, Paul reflected as he lay in bed contemplating the evening's events. With a sudden groan he recalled that he hadn't fixed his puncture.

Muttering, he buried his head deeper into the pillow. Yes, not one of his better expeditions, not by a long chalk.

A week after the shed escapade, Mrs Carr barged into the kitchen, catching her son picking at a newly baked jam sponge. 'Ah, there you are. Now leave it alone. You're as bad as your father.' She smacked his hand away as he reached for more. 'Oh, by the way, I want a word with you. I was just talking to Mrs Hughes. Do you what she found hidden in Tubby's bedroom?'

'No, what?' Paul stopped chewing.

'One of those books – you know, those rude ones.'

Paul pulled a face. 'No, I don't know.'

'The ones full of naked women. She was right upset, I can tell you.'

The penny dropped, and Paul's mind flashed back to their footplate incursion. The sly devil! His amused expression was quickly noticed by his mother. 'You don't know anything about it, do you, Paul?'

'Me, Mum? Course not. You know me, Mum.'

'Yes, I do know you, and if I catch you with anything like that in this house, you'll be out on your ear.'

'Yes, Mum.'

'Oh, don't go calling round for Tubby – he's being kept in for a week.'

'Yes, Mum.' Paul left the kitchen. There was no need to go and to see Tubby. He would see him tomorrow at school, and gleefully rubbed his hands in anticipation. Tomorrow looked like being a good day.

4

SOUTHERN STEAM

Paul slumped in his mother's favourite armchair, seduced by the warmth of the blazing coal fire. Staring past Buster dozing by the hearth, he became mesmerised by the dancing flames, and began to dream, his fantasy transporting him to the footplate of a streamlined 'A4' 'Pacific'. Paul looked around the cab, scrutinising the controls, before occupying the vacant driver's seat. He watched intently as the fireman carefully inspected the fire, using his shovel to deflect the glare from the incandescent flames, before strategically placing six rounds of coal in the firebox. Fully satisfied, he wiped his brow, checked the steam pressure gauge, and lit a cigarette. Paul looked at his watch – two minutes behind

chedule. He opened the regulator, and increased speed. 'The Flying Scotsman' would arrive ahead of time, he would see o that!

Silver Fox raced on, careering past a stationary goods rain, its crew wildly cheering him on. He altered the cut-off and adjusted the regulator. The exhaust barked – this bank was certainly challenging. 'She's a good 'un!' he yelled. The fireman smiled and after a brief nod continued his efforts, his enthusiasm equalling that of the youthful driver. This really was stirring stuff. *Silver Fox* roared noisily up he bank before charging down the gradient. 110mph! The speedometer flickered and crept upwards. 117mph – wonderful, simply wonderful! Wind tugged his hair and scenic greens combined to form a tangled web of colour. Glancing at the speedometer confirmed that they were about o set a new speed record – 133mph. Wow!

Yelp! Buster noisily awoke from his slumber, waking his young master. Paul blinked and stared angrily at the dog. Buster, you big lump! Why can't you dream somewhere else? You've just ruined mine!'

Buster wagged his tail, before performing a couple of stretches, terminating in a lengthy yawn. I wonder what dogs dream about, thought Paul. Probably cats and dogs, or food. Knowing Buster, it was the latter. His thoughts were interrupted by a call from the kitchen.

'Tea's ready!'

He headed for the kitchen, only to be overtaken by the dog.

Mr Carr slowly ate his fish and chips, glancing occasionally at his wife who, complaining of a headache, picked up the *Liverpool Echo* and began to read. Paul and Joan exchanged glances.

'Must have had a row,' his sister whispered, as Paul crammed his mouth full of chips.

Opposite: In the cab of No 60017 *Silver Fox* – Paul's dream is a reality for his footplateman about to leave Doncaster with the 'White Rose' on 1 December 1962. *Ray Ruffell, Silver Link Publishing collection*

'Yes,' came the mumbled reply. Something brushed against his leg. Buster was under the table – knowing his young master, a chip would soon fall.

'Paul.' Mr Carr eventually spoke. 'Your mother wants me to drive down to London on Saturday to pick up your Auntie Molly.' Paul gasped and stopped eating. 'As you know, she's your mother's only sister,' adding 'Thank God' under his breath. 'She's coming up from Brighton on Saturday morning and I've been asked to meet her at Victoria station at 11 o'clock. I suppose you'll want to come?'

'Do I? Wow!' Paul jumped up, nearly upsetting the table.

His mother turned on him angrily. 'Sit down and don't be so silly. Oh, and finish your tea – I don't enjoy cooking for nothing.'

Excitement flowed through his veins as he visualised 'Battle of Britain' Class locomotives, 'Schools' and 'King Arthurs', not to mention other Southern Region classes.

'Can Philip and Tubby come, Dad?'

'No, there won't be room.'

'Well, just Philip then? Oh, come on Dad, he's only slight.'

'Just as well I'm working, isn't it?' exclaimed Joan, pulling a face at her brother.

Ignoring the banter, Mr Carr wavered. 'Well, only Philip. We'll be in for an early start. I want to leave at 4.30, and if we're late, we're late,' the latter statement not improving his wife's mood.

Rain pelted down forming large pools, reflecting the greyness of the night sky. Grids gurgled and sang as streams of water dashed for freedom, bringing music to the deserted streets. Cycling through the downpour, Paul's one thought was to reach Philip's house. His tyres hissed – just one street and he would be there. Squelching to a halt he dismounted and knocked furiously on his pal's front door. Mrs Wood seemed surprised to see him.

'Hello, Paul. What a night to be out! You're soaked. Come in and take off your mackintosh. Philip, Paul's here!'

'I'm in here.'

Paul entered the front room, finding his pal tinkering with his model railway, and immediately blurted out his news. 'Listen, Phil, my Dad's motoring down to London Victoria station on Saturday to pick up Aunt Molly. Anyway, you can come if you want. The only thing is you will have to be up and at our house for 4.30am.'

'That early? Is Tubby going?'

'No room, I'm afraid – I've already asked.'

Looking thoughtful, Philip adjusted the brushes on his Hornby Dublo 'Castle' locomotive before replying, 'You won't find Victoria so exciting. Not much steam there these days – nearly all electric. Waterloo's much better.'

Paul felt a pang of disappointment. 'Are you coming then?'

'Yes, I'll come. It should be a good day out. I'll have to get someone to do my paper round. Still, I should be able to sort that out.'

Paul breathed a sigh of relief, watching his pal place *Bristol Castle* back on the rails. Seconds later it sped around the track. Philip grunted – most satisfactory. Yes, most satisfactory.

4.00am. Gosh, it was cold. Paul looked at the mosaic pattern of frost covering the window. He shivered and dressed. 5.00am, and approaching Warrington Philip and Paul were chattering like parrots. Warrington Bank Quay station passed – nothing! The chatter continued. Dawn broke as they travelled through Cheshire, then came Staffordshire, before a brief tea stop on the A5. Snoring greeted their arrival in St Albans, Philip the culprit. Mr Carr cursed under his breath as he fought through the capital's traffic. Glancing in his mirror he noted that both his passengers were asleep. Lucky for them, he thought. A clock chimed – 11.00am. He was going to be late.

So this was London Victoria station, the gateway to the continent. Paul was unimpressed. He looked around, observing BR Standard Class 4 tank No 80031 simmering in Platform 2 with a train of empty Bulleid carriages. A profusion of electric multiple units occupied most of the other platforms, and the constant activity reminded Paul of bees servicing a hive.

A Bo-Bo electric locomotive had caught Philip's eye. 'Come on, Paul, let's get some platform tickets.'

'Better tell my Dad first. You go on – I'll meet you under the destination board.'

Aunt Molly and his father chatted in the station cafeteria. His Dad looked shattered, Paul thought. His aunt was of the same opinion, and voiced the fact. 'A good three hours rest, Norman, that's what you need, a good three hours. It really was good of you to pick me up. Heavens, I didn't expect it.'

Impatiently, Paul butted in. 'Dad, are you going to have a three-hour rest before we return?'

Mr Carr knew what was coming – he could read his son like a book. 'Why?'

'Well, Philip and I could catch the Underground to Waterloo. Philip knows the way.'

'We could go for a meal while they're gone,' interrupted his aunt.

Mr Carr hesitated. 'You definitely know the way to Waterloo and back?'

'Yes, Dad, Philip has done it before, honest.'

'Have you enough money, dear?' asked his aunt.

'Yes, thank you. Oh, come on, Dad!'

'Right, it's 11.26 – be back outside this cafe at 2.45, and I mean 2.45, no later.'

'Thanks, Dad! Bye!'

Paul joyfully departed, wondering how to get to Waterloo. Philip paced impatiently below the destination board holding a couple of platform tickets, only to be greeted by his excited pal. 'Listen, Phil, my Dad says we can go to Waterloo, just as long as we are back here by 2.45.'

'Why Waterloo? Why not Liverpool Street or King's Cross?'

'Oh, come on, when do we get to see Southern steam?' His pal pondered – Paul had a point. 'Do you know the way to Waterloo?'

Philip shook his head. 'No, but it should be easy if we follow the Underground map.'

The boys were talking next to E5003, a fairly new Bo-Bo electric locomotive of a class operating on the Southern Region's 750-volt third rail dc system. The locomotive held Philip's attention for some considerable time while he explained the principle of electric traction, ignoring the bored look on the recipient's face.

'Come on, let's go to Waterloo!' exploded Paul.

'Well, all right, but before we go, why don't you get the number of that "Schools" Class on the end of the empty stock? It backed on when you were in the cafe. It's 30925 *Cheltenham**!' shouted Philip, as Paul dashed down the platform. 'I think she's on a special working.'

Paul's sudden exertion brought its reward. *Cheltenham* stood quietly simmering, awaiting her next turn of duty. Good engines, by all accounts. She looked splendid, a powerful workhorse with pleasing lines. His first 'Schools' Class, perhaps an omen of things to come.

The 'Schools' Class were considered by many to be the finest 4-4-0s ever to run in Britain. Fast and powerful, they soon became firm favourites with both drivers and the public.

Cheltenham stood quietly simmering, waiting her next turn of duty.' No 30925 is seen at Charing Cross in about 1952. A. J. Pike OBE, courtesy of Frank Hornby

Hurriedly, the boys crossed the Thames by way of the Underground, a short journey with only one change. On leaving the train Paul remarked how easy it had been. 'Yes,' replied Philip. 'But always check you're on the right line and keep studying the map.'

Briskly they entered Waterloo station. Gosh, it was huge – Philip claimed that it had more than twenty platforms. Paul looked around, dismayed by the vast number of electric multiple units frequenting the station. After purchasing platform tickets, they checked the departure board, noting that a Southampton train was about to leave from Platform 11. The station's central cab road ran alongside the platform and they were delighted to find 'M7' No 30133 at the buffers with a train of empty carriages. Originally designed for light passenger duties in 1897, the 'M7s' proved to be extremely versatile, hence their longevity. Increased maintenance costs together with the introduction of the newer BR Standard tanks, compounded their demise, many having been withdrawn.

Paul studied the 'M7' intently, his concentration broken by Philip's urgent cry. Groups of spotters were racing down the platform, the train engine having be sighted. 'Merchant Navy' Class No 35018 *British India Line** ghosted onto the stock, escaping steam engulfing the small group of spotters running alongside the engine. Paul beamed, having increased his collection. Philip, however, was unimpressed. 'They're a damn sight better now that they've got rid of all that streamlining and oil bath nonsense. She's got a wonderful boiler, and I believe they're putting up some exceptional performances. Prior to rebuilding, they could be erratic and unreliable – some even caught fire!' Paul hung on Philip's every word – after all, he certainly knew his stuff.

Introduced by the Southern Railway as a mixed-traffic design during the Second World War, the streamlined 'Merchant Navy', and lighter 'West Country' and 'Battle of Britain', Bulleid 'Pacifics' possessed a unique form of chain-driven valve gear, encased in an oil bath. Other nove

A panoramic view of Waterloo station from the top of the Shell Tower on London's South Bank. The date is 21 December 1965, and the 13.30 service to Bournemouth and Weymouth is pulling out. *Ray Ruffell, Silver Link Publishing collection*

One of the versatile 'M7' 0-4-4Ts, No 30249, passes the signal box at Waterloo having brought in the empty stock for the 'Atlantic Coast Express' on 5 February 1963. *Ray Ruffell, Silver Link Publishing collection*

and innovative ideas also featured in the new locomotives. However, running and maintenance problems raised doubts about their reliability, resulting in the rebuilding of the entire 'Merchant Navy' Class from 1956 onwards. Walschaerts valve gear replaced the original, and the rebuilt locomotives took on a more conventional appearance. Many of the lighter 'Pacifics' were similarly treated. They frequently reached speeds in excess of 90 miles per hour and were highly regarded by footplate crews. It is a pity that such excellent locomotives did not enjoy a longer life. One cannot help wondering why the rebuilt versions were not transferred to the London Midland Region, where there was a shortage of powerful express passenger engines.

A typical trainspotter's photograph showing a 'Merchant Navy' 'Pacific' arriving at Waterloo in May 1964. Taken by 16-year-old Frank Davies, using his new Brownie camera, how many readers took similar pictures? My first efforts were poor in comparison, as I usually missed the chimney or the subject was out of focus. It took quite a while to perfect your art, and if you were lucky enough to achieve that perfect shot you immediately showed it to your classmates. Who's a clever boy! *Frank Davies*

No 35018 waited patiently under clear signals, anxious to be off. Suddenly the shrill blast of an inspector's whistle announced her departure. Paul watched as her driver released the brakes and opened the regulator, resulting in a brief wheel slip. Clouds of steam gushed from the cylinder drain cocks, then, with the 'M7' pushing at the rear, she glided effortlessly out of the platform.

The sight of former GWR '57XX' pannier tank No 9672, hauling a parcels van, took them by surprise. Eyes were diverted from the departing express – even Philip was nonplussed. 'What's she doing here?' he muttered, unaware that Nine Elms shed had a small allocation of these versatile tank engines.

Normality returned with the late arrival of BR Standard Class 5 No 73117 *Vivien* on a semi-fast. Several doors slammed open, and hordes of football supporters jumped from the moving train, wildly rushing down the platform,

Nine Elms shed had a small allocation of ex-GWR tank engines, not normally at home on the Southern Region. 0-6-0PT No 9770 stands beside streamlined 'West Country' 'Pacific' No 34043 *Combe Martin* at Waterloo on 6 July 1961. 'Dignity and impudence' is how the photographer described the pair! *Ray Ruffell, Silver Link Publishing collection*

scattering staff and waiting passengers. Many of the Standard class were allocated to the London Midland Region, but remained unnamed.

Minutes later, an excited cheer rang out as 'King Arthur' Class No 30765 *Sir Gareth* reversed under the station roof towards the semi-fast's stock. She quickly coupled up, and her driver waited impatiently for the platform signal to come off, anxiously checking his watch before staring down the platform as the train rapidly filled with scurrying passengers. What a cop – Paul's first 'King Arthur', absolutely brilliant. Wow!

After a long whistle *Sir Gareth* roared out of the platform bound for Basingstoke, Paul's eyes following her every move as the winter sunlight highlighted the departing express. *Sir Gareth* quickly disappeared, her exhaust fading as she rounded the curve leading to Vauxhall.

The 'King Arthur' Class were the most famous express passenger engines associated with the former Southern Railway. Introduced by Urie, Chief Mechanical Engineer of the London & South Western Railway, in 1918, the design was later modified by Maunsell in 1923, producing a highly successful passenger locomotive capable of handling the heavy expresses to the West of England. Scrapping commenced in the late 1950s, the names from the original LSWR engines being transferred to the BR Standard Class 5 locomotives operating on the Southern Region. Nine Elms-based No 73117 *Vivien* had been so treated.

Platform 11 provided a good vantage point, a popular location for local trainspotters, huddled at the end, with Philip and Paul quickly swelling their ranks. Resting in the adjacent bay, 'M7' No 30133 simmered quietly, her crew enjoying a mug of tea, ignoring the spotters' adulation.

Unrebuilt Bulleid 'West Country' 'Pacific' No 34102

Right: An original 'King Arthur': No 30777 *Sir Lamiel* awaits preservation at Fratton shed on 21 July 1964. The locomotive is now part of the National Collection. *Ray Ruffell, Silver Link Publishing collection*

Above: The names of former Southern Railway 'King Arthur' locomotives were transferred to the new BR Standard 4-6-0s used on the Southern Region of BR. At Waterloo on Sunday 7 May 1961, this is No 73118 *King Hodegrance*, a name formerly carried by No 30739. *Ray Ruffell, Silver Link Publishing collection*

Lapford steamed in with a Bournemouth train, creating fresh buzz of excitement. Joined by other spotters, Paul an Philip raced to Platform 13 to examine the new arrival, Pau preferring the streamlined unrebuilt version and voicing th fact. Even Philip seemed pleased, having made an importar cop. Soon they were sprinting to the end of the platform 'M7' No 30133 having taken charge of the empty stock She disappeared towards Clapham carriage sidings and the returned to Platform 11.

'We've really slipped up,' voiced Philip, after conversation with a couple of local lads. 'Apparently mos of the regular spotters catch a train to Clapham Junctio station. You can see all engine movements in and out c Waterloo, plus freight traffic.'

Paul shrugged. 'We wouldn't have had time. We have t be back at a quarter to three. Perhaps we can do that nex time.'

Unrebuilt 'West Country' 'Pacific' No 34102 *Lapford* heads throug Clapham Junction hauling the 12.39 Waterloo-Basingstoke semi-fa service. *Frank Hornby*

Philip grimaced and shook his head, adding, 'They also told me that a special boat train is due to arrive at any minute from Southampton.' In anticipation he turned towards the station throat, only to see the pannier tank heading for Vauxhall. A distant whistle signified the arrival of BR Standard Class 3 tank engine No 82014 with a train of empty carriages, causing major disappointment. Where was the special?

BR Standard Class 3 2-6-2T No 82014 arrives at Clapham Junction with a train of empty carriages from Waterloo. *Ray Ruffell, Silver Link Publishing Collection*

Eight minutes passed before 'Lord Nelson' Class No 30855 *Robert Blake* majestically coasted past the station's large signal box and into the platform, causing a flurry of excitement. Grinding to a halt, she was instantly surrounded by excited spotters. Paul stood in front of the engine, pointing to her enormous smokebox and boiler. She looked massive when viewed from that angle, and Paul was astonished by her bulk. Philip tapped him on the shoulder, shouting, 'A a class they've never been a complete success. Still, she's wonderful sight.' He prattled on until the locomotive's safet valves blew off, drowning all further conversation.

Retreating down the platform, Paul remarked, 'You don't think much of Southern engines, do you, Phil?'

Philip smiled. 'Well, I'm a Stanier fan.'

'But even he made mistakes. What about the "Jubilee" class? When introduced, they were hardly a roaring success.

'No, but the "Duchess" "Pacifics" are masterpieces Works of art.'

'Paul stood in front of the engine, pointing to her enormous smokebo and boiler. She looked massive when viewed from that angle...' A strikin view of 'Lord Nelson' Class No 30855 *Robert Blake* at Eastleigh shed o 24 July 1961. *Ray Ruffell, Silver Link Publishing collection*

'I bet Sir Nigel Gresley or Oliver Bulleid wouldn't agree.'

His pal's eyes twinkled. 'I suppose you're right – they all ave their merits.'

When introduced by the Southern Railway in 1926, the Lord Nelson' Class locomotives were claimed to be the most owerful locomotives in the UK. The cranks were set to roduce a new power stoke every one-eighth of a revolution, hus eight beats were audible, instead of the normal four. adly they never lived up to expectations, prompting Oliver ulleid to introduce various modifications, improving their erformance. They had a reputation for being difficult to re, and were largely overshadowed by the Bulleid 'Pacifics', sing many of their former duties to the newer locomotives.

'West Country' No 34102 *Lapford* backed slowly out f the station, increasing speed as she headed for Nine lms shed. A quiet spell followed, and eighteen minutes assed before the arrival of rebuilt 'Battle of Britain' Class ocomotive No 34052 *Lord Dowding*. They watched as

the dying months of Southern Region steam, 'Battle of Britain' 'Pacific' o 34052 *Lord Dowding* arrives at Woking with a up Salisbury commuter rvice on 12 May 1967. *Ray Ruffell, Silver Link Publishing collection*

'U' Class 2-6-0 No 31627 stands at Guildford station with the 5.24pr service to Reading on 14 October 1963. *Ray Ruffell, Silver Link Publishir collection*

she cautiously reversed into Platform 8 to couple up to Salisbury train. The engine simmered quietly as the crev prepared to leave, her blower producing a jet of light gre smoke, which quickly darkened as the sound of the firemans shovel reverberated around the cab. Whistles blew, cylinder hissed, and she puffed out, hauling nine packed carriages.

Wearily the boys sat down on a trolley, their early star taking effect. Paul glanced at his watch. Nearly time to go Yawning and stretching, he stared at his notebook. Still tim for another cop.

As if on cue, 'L1' Class No 31757 arrived, piloting Clas 'U' No 31618* on a semi-fast. Amazing! Even Philip jumpe up. Gosh, an 'L1' and a 'U'! Wow! Paul was overjoyed. The watched them steam past, feasting on their every movemen Pointing at the 'L1', Philip yelled, 'They're an excellent 4-4 0s! Much better than the LMS Class 2 versions!' What Philip praising a Southern class? He must be slipping!

The sands of time were running out. 2.20pm arrived and with it their departure. Glancing back, they made their way to the Underground. It certainly had been time well spent, giving them a taste of Southern steam. Speeding along on the Underground, Philip broached a question that had been puzzling him all day.

'Paul, I know it's none of my business, but why has your Dad got to drive all this way to pick up your aunt? I mean, why couldn't she catch a train to Liverpool. It seems crazy to me.'

His pal hesitated. 'Well, don't say anything, but apparently she's a very nervous person and can't travel far on her own. Even when she came up from Brighton, Aunt Molly had a friend travelling with her as far as Victoria. I heard my Mum say she had had a nervous breakdown about two years ago. That's why my Dad picked her up. I know he didn't want to. It's an awful long drive.'

Philip nodded and his eyes wandered to the Underground map. They were nearly at Victoria.

Mr Carr grunted. They were on time – amazing. Pity really – the drive back felt most unwelcome.

'Enjoyed yourselves?'

'Yes, thanks,' came the chorus.

'Right, well, let's be off then. Aunt Molly's in the car.'

Philip shot one last glance at Platform 2. Nothing. As if there would be – he'd only checked seconds before. A minor breeze greeted their exit, fresh air at last – or was it? The traffic buzzed noisily, getting near to the Christmas rush, thought Mr Carr – I must be mad. Still, it had provided the boys with an interesting afternoon. His Morris Minor beckoned. Once seated, the chatter began. Oh no, not trains again! Sighing, he switched on the ignition, revved the engine and slowly edged into the traffic – heavens, he was tired! Glancing around, he noticed Aunt Molly clinging to the interior strap. Here we go again, he mused. They were on their way.

5
CHESTER, SHREWSBURY – AND WOLVERHAMPTON?

Christmas had long passed. Spring had arrived and with a new decade, historically momentous for steam and for the spotters. Slowly but surely they would witness the elimination of steam from British Railways operations. Modernisation was on the march, and numerous new diesel locomotives were being manufactured by various companies, adding to a perplexing mix. They seemed to be establishing themselves all too quickly. However, there were failures much welcomed by a troubled Paul.

Spring sunshine shone through the classroom window. Paul basked in it, meticulously studying his new Ian Allan *Combined* while shooting disconcerting glances at Philip, sitting at the adjacent desk.

'Look at all these new diesel classes, Phil – everyone seems to be making them! Just think of all the new "Blin Niners" now entering service. I ask you, why keep building all these different types of diesels – it's just plain stupid.'

Philip shrugged. Mr Piggot stirred, his concentration broken by the muttering of a distant voice. Shoving a recently confiscated *Men Only* magazine into the top drawer, he glanced around the class. Someone wasn't working and he wanted to know why. His eyes rested on Paul.

'Finished, Carr?'

The lad looked a picture of innocence. 'Yes, Sir.'

'Right, let's have a look at what you've done – bring out, will you?'

Picking up his painting, he walked towards Mr Piggot, or 'Piglet' as he was popularly known, feeling not for the first time the class's attention riveted on his frame. Art wasn't

Paul's field really – now woodwork, that was different. The teacher scrutinised his work with astonishment. He'd asked the boys to paint a country scene, and somehow this idiot had managed to paint a railway tunnel into the bottom right-hand corner. What a mess!

'Carr, that is one of the worst paintings I've ever seen.' Paul blushed. 'Do you know that the whole thing has only taken you twenty minutes? Let's hope you improve with age, otherwise when you leave school the only painting you'll be doing is that of houses.'

'Just like Hitler,' voiced Sammy Price, causing ripples of mirth amongst the front row.

'Wrong – Hitler could paint. Carr, sit down and start again.' He wanted to return to his magazine – it really was most interesting.

The clanging of the bell shattered the silence, and with a screech chairs were pushed back as a mass of bodies noisily left the room. Paul battled towards the door, searching for Tubby. Where was he? Ah, as expected, heading for the dinner queue.

While painting, Paul had been planning another trip. Philip hadn't been impressed – now he could outline and explain his plan to Tubby.

After lunch, Paul assembled the class's small fraternity of trainspotters. Philip was noticeably absent, having gone home for lunch. Badger, Pearson, Murphy, Roberts and Thompson listened as he enthusiastically outlined his plan. What about a trip to Wolverhampton Low Level station via Chester and Shrewsbury? They could stop off at the latter town before proceeding to Wolverhampton. Imagine all the ex-Great Western engines to be seen – steam still dominated that route. They were all interested – the only problem was money.

'How much will it cost?' Roberts asked in a tentative tone.

'I don't know yet – couple of pounds, I suppose.'

'Count me out,' Roberts said glumly.

'Me too, I'm broke. Mind you, I'll go if someone lends

me the money. I'll pay them back, honest.' Murphy looked apprehensively at his classmates.

Paul glanced out of the window, and silence reigned Murphy wasn't very popular and it showed. 'Well, that's then,' he huffed, storming off with his pal Thompson.

'Who's in?' Paul demanded, watching Murphy bitterly complaining to his pal. By the look of it Thompson couldn't help him either. Pearson nodded his approval. 'I'm in,' said Badger. Tubby he knew was already going, but Philip was proving difficult – he would have to work on him later. 'Right then, let's make the arrangements.'

The following Saturday five trainspotters stood on a desolate platform at Mossley Hill station – Badger, Tubby, Paul and Pearson, who had arrived with his nine-year-old brother much to their annoyance. Philip had finally declined preferring to save his money for a trip to York, the lack of diesels proving decisive.

Fuming inwardly, Paul glared at Pearson's younger brother and pointed to the bored-looking lad. 'What did you bring him for?'

Pearson shrugged. 'My Mum made me,' he bleated. 'It was the only way she'd give me the money to go. She said she wanted a bit of peace for a change.'

'Don't we all?' rasped Paul.

According to Badger, Pearson's younger brother Eric had a fearsome reputation – now they would have to watch him constantly. It could ruin their day. He was beginning to have doubts about the whole venture and seethed even more. All he needed now was for Tubby and Pearson to start bickering. He shuddered and began to feel dismal. The old station had all but disappeared since his last visit. a temporary booking office having sprung up on Platform 2. It lacked atmosphere and substance, being replaced by a compact modern nondescript building, the flower tubs, coal fires and gleaming brass lost for ever. Electrification was swiftly eradicating the steam age and its associated Victorian nfrastructure. Despondency set in and he was soon in a mood.

'Here she comes!' yelled Tubby. 'We've got a Caprotti standard Class 5.'

No 73129* put up an indifferent performance, arriving n Chester four minutes late, a signal check at Frodsham not helping matters. Apart from the sighting of former LNER Class 'O4' No 63598 at Mickle Trafford with an unfitted freight, nothing special had been sighted. Speke shed failed o produce its customary row of withdrawn 'Super Ds'. On lighting they quickly obtained day returns for Shrewsbury before making their way to the former Great Western Railway terminus of this busy station.

Trains, both passenger and goods, paraded through continually, so they were fully occupied as they awaited the Birkenhead to Paddington express. LMS 'Crab' No 42765* wheezed by on a freight, quickly followed by Midland 4F No 44445, and No 45556 *Nova Scotia*, a grubby 'Jubilee'. No 3665, a former GWR '57XX' pannier tank, crept antalisingly onto the scene from the direction of Chester West engine shed; however, the sight of an express passenger locomotive scuttling about in the distance prompted the boys to ignore the pannier. The new arrival appeared to be a 'Castle', creating ripples of excitement – perhaps she would pull their train.

Feeling buoyant, Paul leaned over the edge of the platform and peered optimistically towards Chester West shed, Tubby anxiously listening to his report. 'Looks like a "28XX", and a "43XX". I can't be sure though, they're too far away. Damn that road bridge – it's blocking the view.'

'No namers?' enquired Tubby, wobbling dangerously on the edge of the platform.

'Doesn't look like it.'

A distant whistle signified the arrival of their train. Heads craned in eager anticipation, followed by moans of disappointment as No 42077, a filthy Fairburn tank, clanked in, its appearance contrasting sharply with that of

Among the engines seen at Chester was 'Crab' 2-6-0 No 42765. This locomotive, which can still be seen today in preservation, was photographed at Birkenhead shed on 26 June 1965. *The late W. G. Boyden, courtesy of Frank Hornby*

'Black Five' 4-6-0 No 45250 waits to leave Chester with the 08.03 service to Crewe on 19 June 1965. *Ray Ruffell, Silver Link Publishing collection*

On 13 April 1965 guard and driver confer before the departure of the 7.10pm service from Chester to London Paddington, which 'Black Five' No 45282 will take as far as Shrewsbury. *Ray Ruffell, Silver Link Publishing collection*

'Paul ... peered optimistically towards Chester West shed... "Looks like '28XX'..." It is – 2-8-0 No 3855 stands next to '5700' Class 0-6-0PT No 3794 at Chester West on 3 March 1960. *Ron Herbert*

the gleaming chocolate and cream stock.

The station announcements blared as they scramble[d] into the still moving train. Once aboard they immediatel[y] searched for a convenient compartment in which to deposi[t] their bags. Paul called to Pearson, 'This looks promising, having spotted a compartment occupied solely by a vica[r]. 'He should keep young Eric in check.'

'There's a courting couple in the next one. Come o[n] let's go in there! It should be a good laugh!' Tubby voice[d] gleefully. Crack – the adjoining compartment door slamme[d] shut, indicating that they were not welcome.

'Must have heard you, Tubby. Come on, this will do,' called Paul. Impassively the vicar watched them enter, the[n] continued to glance at his book. 'Excuse me. Will it be a[ll] right if we leave our bags here while we trainspot?' Pau[l] peered into the vicar's face and, without waiting for a repl[y] deposited his bag by the window. A small collection of bag[s] rapidly assembled containing an array of thermos flasks an[d] bottles, Tubby's bag being the exception. How did he kno[w] the vicar was honest, Tubby remarked – he might eat h[is] sandwiches – bringing groans from his pals.

Badger looked at the vicar. 'Are you interested in trains[?]'

'No, I can't say that I am,' came the blunt reply.

'Trust us to get a vicar that's not train mad,' whispere[d] Paul.

'Blimey, I thought they all liked trains, just like Eri[c] Treacy,' replied Tubby in a puzzled tone. 'Perhaps he's not [a] vicar at all – perhaps he's an actor or something.'

'Don't be daft! Come on, let's see what's going to pull u[s] to Shrewsbury.'

Noting that Eric was safely tucked away in the corne[r] reading the *Beano*, they departed, after instructing him t[o] await their return and keep an eye on the bags. The latte[r] remark caused the vicar some amusement.

Badger was already on the platform watching the elusiv[e] 'Castle' back onto their train. 'Wow, it's 7004 *Eastno[r] Castle*!'

'Cop, cop!' cried Paul. 'Now you'll really see some reworks.'

With a dull thud the engine and carriages combined, the engine's polished paintwork matching that of the stock. Paul slowly walked alongside the engine, meticulously examining every detail, exhilarated at the thought of travelling behind such a handsome locomotive. Looking at his companions confirmed that his pleasure was equally shared.

Tubby looked at his watch and grabbed Paul's arm. 'Come on, let's get aboard – she'll be off soon.'

Unwillingly he reboarded, followed by the others, noisily making their way back to the 'vicarage', as Pearson had christened the compartment. The sight of three vicars and no Eric provided a major shock. Once he had sufficiently recovered, Paul enquired as to Eric's whereabouts.

'Castle' at Chester. In June 1964 filthy No 7012 *Barry Castle* (the author's namesake) waits at signals en route to Chester Midland shed, Chester West having closed in April 1960. Representing one of the last batch to be constructed after the Second World War, she has not been modified with a double chimney, unlike her sister *Eastnor Castle*. *The late J.W. Sutherland*

'Muttered something about this being a non-smoker,' voiced one of the new arrivals, clearly disturbed.

'Thank you, vicar, we'll find him.'

The train jolted – they were on their way. Now all the had to do was find the little sod, as Paul politely put it Tubby had other things on his mind – Paul caught him tryin to peep under the blinds hastily pulled down in the adjacen compartment.

'Wonder what they're doing,' smirked his pal.

'Playing chess,' came the sarcastic reply.

'Oh, surely not – I bet they're…' He never finished th sentence. A cry rang out – Eric had been found.

'"County"!' shouted Badger just as Paul sped along th corridor. No 1013 *County of Dorset* glided past the carriag door as he fumbled with the window strap – blast, it wa jammed! He cursed and it tumbled down, the inrushing air sharp reminder that the train was constantly gathering speed A compartment door slammed behind him. Leaning out, h could just see the tender of the 'County' spilling water as sh disappeared around the curve. Turning forward proved t be a disaster – smuts entered his eyes, forcing a rapid retrea By chance he encountered Pearson holding a smoulderin Woodbine – he stepped aside while it was deposited out c the window.

'One of my Dad's,' he muttered.

Paul's anger abated; he felt suddenly sorry for Pearson Fancy having a brother like that, he mused.

Chester's suburbs gradually disappeared, and th rhythmic exhaust of the 'Castle' changed to staccato coinciding with a loss of pace – Gresford Bank beckoned One of the vicars had appeared armed with a tape-recorde to capture the unique sound of the 'Castle' storming th steep gradient. At last, a vicar interested in trains – it wa enough to make one become a man of the cloth, commente Tubby, after having helped the gentleman with his task.

Paul was still smiling at the remark as they storme through Chirk, passing '28XX' No 3822* in the process

They were racing now and it was wonderful. Gobowen produced No 7822 *Foxcote Manor** and No 7414, a small '74XX' Class pannier tank, on a push-and-pull, a toy train by any standards. Philip would have enjoyed this, Paul thought – pity he hadn't come. He could picture him leaning out of the carriage window wearing those ridiculous goggles – if French engine drivers wore them, why not him? Paul wished for a pair at that very moment, on examining his sooty and tearful face. A '56XX' Class engine flashed by, then a 'WD'. Excited cries rang out – they had reached Shrewsbury.

What a busy station! On first appearance trains seemed to be everywhere. Leaning out of the window, Paul could see that they were about to pass a "Mickey" and a "Royal Scot". Weaving continuously across the carriage, the boys shouted out the numbers, having been joined by the equally enthusiastic vicar.

'45305* ... 46131 *The Royal Warwickshire Regiment*...' Paul groaned – he'd seen her before. '"45XX" tank 5535* piloting 7922 *Salford Hall*...' A cop! Jabbering loudly, they

Rushing through Chirk station on 16 August 1961 is BR Standard Class 5 No 73049 on an up freight. *Ron Herbert*

More than a dozen ex-GWR '28XX' 2-8-0s have been preserved, including No 3822, seen at Chirk. An anonymous member of the class awaits preservation in Eastleigh Works yard on 16 January 1966. *Ray Ruffell, Silver Link Publishing collection*

Ex-GWR 4-6-0 No 7822 *Foxcote Manor*, spotted at Gobowen, was another engine to pass into preservation. Sister loco No 7813 *Freshford Manor*, seen here at Guildford with a Reading service on 11 December 1963, was not so lucky... *Ray Ruffell, Silver Link Publishing collection*

umbled onto the platform just as No 6853 *Morehampton Grange* trundled through on a fitted freight.

Paul grinned. 'Told you it would be great here! Come on, et's go to the south end.'

They bade the vicar farewell, and marched off, Paul urging ahead with Tubby bringing up the rear.

Derby-based 'Jubilee' No 45618 *New Hebrides* has just arrived at Shrewsbury with an express from the West of England on 23 June 1962, becoming the focus for the group of spotters gathered on Platform 4. It was nice to take the weight off your feet, and platform trolleys provided a wonderful observation platform. In the background one can see the large signal box at the station's southern throat. *John Hunt*

The group emerged from the station's gloomy interior into sunlight and sat down on an aptly placed platform trolley, their faces turned towards *Eastnor Castle*, an impatient greyhound anxious to be off. After a long blast on her whistle, she hissed into action, sniffing her way over the points, the engine's rhythmic bark once more challenged the morning air. In less than a minute she was gone, steam and smoke a fleeting monument to her passing. Silence returned and the boys felt a sudden loss.

During their lifetime the 'Castle' locomotives had earned a reputation that had little equal. Held in high esteem by both running staff and footplate crews, these engines became a legend. Free-running and powerful, they handled the bulk of the Western Region's expresses, frequently hauling such famous trains as the 'Bristolian' and the 'Cheltenham Flyer'.

Three wonderful and pulsating hours passed. 'Halls' 'Granges' and 'Castles' were seen, as well as the more familiar 'Jubilees', 'Royal Scots', 'Black Fives' and 'Patriots'. Alas, no 'King' Class locomotives presented themselves, prompting Paul to call a conference.

'Right, who's coming to Wolverhampton?' No one spoke. 'Oh, come on, you lot – don't you want to see some "Kings"? he cried impatiently. 'There will be some there you can bet on it!'

The free-running and powerful ex-GWR 'Castle' 4-6-0s had a fine a reputation, popular with both running staff and footplate crews. No 5014 *Goodrich Castle* returns to the loco depot at Taunton on 9 March 1962 *Ray Ruffell, Silver Link Publishing collection*

Badger looked at the faces of his companions before replying. 'Listen, Paul, we're just as likely to see them here as at Wolverhampton. Ask those spotters over there – they say that "Kings" appear here. If we wait long enough we're bound to see one.'

'I wouldn't guarantee it,' snapped Paul.

Badger gave him a thoughtful look. 'You said it yourself this is a great spot. Tell you what – if you want to go, go!

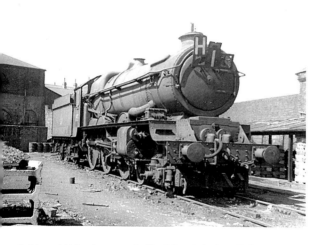

A sad sight at Wolverhampton Stafford Road shed in 1963: withdrawn 'King' Class 4-6-0 No 6012 *King Edward VI* presents a forlorn spectacle as she awaits her final journey to the scrapyard. Interestingly, she still displays reporting numbers on her smokebox door, a Western Region practice not appreciated by spotters, as their presence completely masked the smokebox number. The writer recalls a rail trip from Torquay to Crewe during the summer of 1959 when practically every approaching engine carried these large numbers, causing endless frustration. Torture indeed!
John Burnett

We'll wait for you here.' Heads nodded in agreement.

'That's good of you,' Paul retorted. He looked at Tubby 'What about you?'

Tubby looked at the others and shrugged, then pretending he'd spotted something of interest, walked down the platform.

'You lousy lot – I mean, we all agreed...' His anger overflowed and he stormed off, ignoring their shouts. Pearson raced after him, frantically tugging his arm and pointing down the platform. Spotters were shouting and jumping with delight, before running towards an approaching train. Seconds later No 6024 *King Edward I** drifted into the platform with the 'Cambrian Coast Express'. What a sight! Paul just stared, watching Tubby lumbering along the platform, trying to keep up with the engine. Badger gestured frantically for them to join him, before grabbing Eric and running down the platform. Paul and Pearson sprinted to join their pals, who had practically disappeared in the crowd of enthusiasts milling around the engine. Minutes later she

In happier days, No 6024 *King Edward I* stands at Plymouth Laira shed in June 1956. Fortunately, the loco survived Barry scrapyard and now runs once more in preservation. *A. J. Pike OBE, courtesy of Frank Hornby*

had uncoupled, standing patiently in front of a discerning audience. Paul's joy was complete, and he quickly abandoned his plan to travel to Wolverhampton.

Once described as an enlarged version of the 'Castle' Class, the 'Kings' were introduced in 1927, the GWR claiming them as Britain's most powerful express passenger locomotives. Fitted with double chimneys and improved draughting in the late 1950s, they were now at their peak, being by far the largest express passenger locomotives on the Western Region. Dieselisation soon caught up with them, however, and it seems a great pity that such handsome and

The 'Kings' were still capable of remarkable performances in their twilight years in the early 1960s. No 6021 *King Richard II* stands at Leamington Spa station after an 85mph dash from Banbury with the 13-coach 9.10am from Paddington on 27 October 1961. *Ray Ruffell, Silver Link Publishing Collection*

efficient locomotives went to the breaker's yard within a few years of Paul's sighting.

Receiving word that a 'Manor' was reversing onto the rear of the express prompted another platform dash. Tubby breathlessly flopped onto a platform trolley, exhausted by his recent exertion. Once recovered, he rejoined his pals, who were watching the 'Manor' couple up. Hunger soon got the better of him, however, so he returned to the trolley and sat down. He then opened his bag, producing a bottle of Tizer, a sausage roll and a copy of *Trains Illustrated* magazine. Calling Pearson, he opened the magazine, pointing out a couple of picture cops between bouts of eating. Together, they flicked through the pages, Pearson commenting on the various photographs as Paul looked on. Not to be outdone, Badger produced a copy of *Meccano Magazine* and showed them a diagram of the layout he was about to build in the spare room, creating a wealth of questions.

The conversation subsided as Shrewsbury-based BR Standard Class 5 No 73096* steamed in on a semi-fast from Hereford. The Western Region had painted its BR mixed traffic Standard classes Brunswick green, a colour normally applied to express passenger locomotives. Badger recalled having seen Shrewsbury-based No 73094 at Manchester Victoria the previous week. Paul did not doubt his claim, having witnessed green-liveried BR 'Standards 5s' at Edge Hill shed.

No 7802 *Bradley Manor** fairly sparkled, a credit to the cleaners at Aberystwyth shed, in the former Cambrian section. Western Region engines were always cleaner than their London Midland counterparts, whose sheds struggled to find sufficient cleaning staff. Joined by Tubby and Pearson, Paul watched her depart. With no sign of a slip, the 5ft 8in driving wheels of the 'Manor' slowly engaged the greasy rails, then she glided effortlessly out of the station, her safety valves discharging a whisper of steam as she negotiated the junction leading to the Cambrian Coast. The sight of the 'King' clanking down the platform halted further interest in

Standard 5' 4-6-0 No 73096, complete with reporting numbers, blows off prior to departure from Exeter St David's during the 1950s; two schoolboys are taking a keen interest in proceedings. No 73096, subsequently preserved, appears to be in black livery; however, this Shrewsbury-based engine was later repainted Brunswick green by the Western Region, and the author recalls seeing her at Edge Hill shed in ex-works condition. *Author's collection*

the departing express. Her crew obediently stopped her at the platform starting signal, then seconds later she snorted off towards Shrewsbury engine shed.

The arrival of gleaming Bristol-based 'Patriot' No 5519 *Lady Godiva* on a lengthy parcels train caused a major sensation. After carefully threading her way across the station throat, she drifted through the station, heading for Crewe. Whoops of joy echoed down the platform, Paul literally jumping in sheer delight – she rarely visited the North West.

Another preserved engine, No 7802 *Bradley Manor*, is seen durin its working days at Ellesmere at the head of the 12.10pm Welshpoo Manchester Piccadilly service on 18 August 1962. *The late J. M. Tolso courtesy of Frank Hornby*

Paul now decided to visit the gents, somewhat fearfu of what he might miss. Rushing down the platform, h reflected on the day's events. His notebook contained th numbers of former GWR '51XX', '22XX', '43XX', '56XX' '57XX', '45XX' and '28XX' classes, together with 'Halls 'Granges', 'Manors' and the solitary 'King' and 'County The latter tally increased when No 1003 *County of Wil* arrived with a Birkenhead express. Having heard the soun of the arriving train, Paul hastily emerged from the toile still fastening his braces, to add another cop to his growin tally. Not the most popular of classes, the 'Counties' wer nevertheless a modern mixed-traffic design, introduce in 1945. The recent addition of a double chimney vastl improved their performance, and they were impressive looking machines.

One class remained elusive – no 'Dukedogs' had appeared. Paul desperately hoped to see one of these hybrids. Sadly it would be his only disappointment; only a few of the class remained, having been replaced by newer locomotives.

The usual batch of 'Jubilees' and 'Royal Scots' produced no great surprises, although Tubby increased his collection with the arrival of 'Royal Scot' No 46167 *The Hertfordshire Regiment* and 'Jubilee' Nos 45558 *Manitoba*, 45686 *St Vincent* and 45631 *Tanganyika*, the latter in ex-works condition.

Eric on the whole had been well-behaved, a fact grudgingly conceded by Badger. Fatigued, the youngster was soon asleep. Deciding to return, they boarded the 5.30pm Paddington to Birkenhead train, aptly pulled by 'Castle' No 5061 *Earl of Birkenhead*, the engine crew producing a stirring performance to arrive at Chester ahead of time. Wearily they changed, boarding a local train home. Even

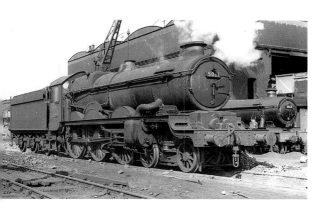

'Castle' Class 4-6-0 No 5061 *Earl of Birkenhead* provided the weary boys with a stirring performance between Shrewsbury and Chester. Here the locomotive is on shed at Old Oak Common on 20 September 1959. *Frank Hornby*

'By the time Ditton Junction arrived a definite plan had taken shape.' In 1960 an unidentified 'Black Five' leaves the fast line hauling a Lourdes special, and drifts onto the slow line prior to stopping at Ditton station. This was an extremely busy junction and Paul would have been keen to spot the industrial engines employed at the various factories alongside the main line between Ditton and Runcorn. *Brian Cassidy*

Paul succumbed to tiredness and sat down, staring out of the window for the remainder of the journey. Dreams of a trip to Sheffield were flickering in his brain. By the time Ditton Junction arrived a definite plan had taken shape. Poking a dozing Tubby, he outlined his plan. Tubby yawned and stared blankly at the rejuvenated face. Oh no, he thought, here we go again.

6
CARLISLE

Kendal bustled with shoppers, resulting in a steady crawl through the town centre. Still, it was not as bad as Lancaster, where traffic had proceeded at walking pace, allowing Paul to leave the car to obtain the numbers of two Stanier 0-4-4 tank engines dumped in a siding outside Lancaster Green Ayre station. He glanced at his notebook: Nos 41903 and 41904 were rare beasts, and their presence had taken him by surprise. Eat your heart out, Tubby, Paul mused, glancing again at the numbers. Introduced by the LMS in 1932, the class of ten engines were more powerful than their Midland Railway predecessors, carrying a 2P power classification. One wonders why they were constructed, as there where plenty of Midland examples available, and the Fowler 2-6-4 tanks introduced five years earlier were far

At Lancaster Green Ayre station in March 1961 Stanier 0-4-4Ts Nos 41903/4 appear in stored condition together with an Ivatt Class 4 'Flying Pig'; Paul copped the pair on his way to Carlisle. Sadly these passenger tank engines went to the breaker's yard. *The late David Frost Collection, courtesy of the GWS, Didcot*

more suited to the requirements of the LMS Motive Power Department.

Lancaster Green Ayre had also produced a withdrawn 'Jinty', together with an electric multiple unit, the line to Morecambe having been electrified by the Midland Railway in 1908, using a 6.5kV ac overhead system. The Midland thus unwittingly paved the way for the introduction of ac overhead electrification on the West Coast Main Line half a century later.

Paul could scarcely believe he was heading for Carlisle. The sudden death of Uncle Bill had shocked the family, and his father was already at his brother's house at Carleton, just outside the city. Uncle Harry's black Humber Hawk began to pick up speed again before slowing, Paul glimpsing again the River Kent, which had noticeably risen since their arrival. Joan fidgeted in the front seat, craning her head as they passed a shoe shop.

'I wouldn't mind looking at the shops,' she murmured, glancing at her mother.

Uncle Harry grimaced. 'Sorry, love, but we are already behind time. You can do your shopping in Carlisle after the funeral.'

Joan sighed. 'I just thought that Kay's might have a factory shop. You could probably pick up a bargain.'

'What is it with you and shoes?' grunted Mrs Carr. 'You've more than enough pairs already.'

The old Humber was warm, spacious and comfortable and Paul began to doze as they left the town and headed for Shap, heavy lorries making progress difficult. It had become increasing gloomy and Joan now wanted to go to the toilet, forcing them to make an impromptu stop at a transport cafe. Heavy rain greeted their exit, low cloud and mist engulfing the fells. Uncle Harry cursed as they rejoined the A6, finding himself at the rear of convoy of assorted vehicles trying to overtake a Ribble Duple half-cab coach. Thankfully the coach driver pulled over to allow them to pass; Paul studied the old Leyland as they did so, drifting steam from its radiator quickly vanishing in the damp atmosphere. Condensation covered the coach windows and many occupants were busily wiping the glass to view their progress. Paul wondered if any of the passengers had noticed the roadside Leyland clock, proudly displaying 'Leyland Motors for all time', its motif enhanced by the inclusion of numerous cat's-eyes. He quite liked old buses, but the Glasgow-bound Leyland was clearly struggling and behind schedule. Not Leyland's finest hour!

Penrith appeared through the gloom, and the rain eased. After overtaking yet another BRS lorry they began to make better progress as they headed towards the former citadel city. Paul studiously searched for plumes of smoke, hoping to locate the West Coast Main Line hidden by the rolling hills.

After another break at a roadside cafe, Uncle Harry relaxed, stating that they would be at the house in half an hour, prompting Paul's mother to rush to a phone box. Paul finished his cup of tea and once again studied his Ian Allan *Combined*, contemplating the funeral and its aftermath. Somehow he had to get into Carlisle, even if he had to walk. Naturally he had a plan – he'd offer to return with his father, who was staying an extra day. After all, he would argue, his Dad could do with some company, and felt sure his parents would agree. Uncle Harry, Joan and his mother planned to return after the funeral, leaving his father to deal with the will – it seemed the perfect ploy. Now all he had to do was pick the right moment.

Carleton at last, and their Morris Minor quickly came into view. The old Humber purred to a halt as Paul's father appeared in the doorway holding a teapot. He knew the way to a woman's heart! Paul helped his uncle with the cases, displaying his best behaviour, anxious not to rock the boat. They were soon enjoying more tea and toast, and discussing the funeral arrangements. Luckily, Mr Carr had managed to obtain a mid-morning cremation, much to the chagrin of various family members, some of whom they had not seen for years. After the service they would go back to the church hall for refreshments, but without Joan, who was hoping to sneak into Carlisle for a couple of hours to do some shopping. Uncle Harry insisted that she be brief as he did not relish tackling the A6 after dark.

Paul could hardly contain his excitement as he ran along Bridge Street and crossed the main running lines, before forking left towards Carlisle Castle. The sudden roar of an approaching express prompted a dash to obtain a viewpoint, his efforts rewarded by the spectacle of a 'Jubilee' fleeing northwards, its cab number indecipherable. He swore and raced on, finding an excellent vantage point north of the castle. Ahead lay the West Coast Main Line and the goods avoiding lines. Wow! Immediately 'J36' No 65293 trundled past hauling a short freight. What wonderful little engines, Paul thought, as he followed her progress southwards. His first cop of the day, and a class previously unseen.

Because it lay at the convergence of several different companies' lines, Carlisle Citadel station was a Mecca for enthusiasts in steam days. Inside the cavernous interior 'Britannia' No 70017 *Arrow* waits impatiently to be off. *Ray Ruffell, Silver Link Publishing collection*

Designed by the North British Railway in 1888, these useful engines had provided excellent service during two World Wars. Twenty-five carried the names of prominent

One of the first locos Paul copped at Carlisle was ex-NBR/LNER 'J36' No 5293. Sister loco No 65260 is seen a little further north at Kipps shed, Glasgow, on 18 August 1955. *The late W. G. Boyden, courtesy of Frank Hornby*

Allied military leaders and also the major battles fought during the Great War. Unnamed No 65293 was a testament to the longevity of the class – would diesels last 70 years, Paul wondered.

'Crab' No 42752 squealed northwards with a coal train, then events became more mundane with the arrival of two 'Black Fives', Paul failing to spot that one carried larger cab numbers, being allocated to Perth. 'J39' No 64888 steamed by with a local passenger train, heading for Carlisle Citadel station, followed by 'Clan' No 72005 *Clan Macgregor* on a parcels train. Seconds later 'A3' No 60041 *Salmon Trout* appeared with an Edinburgh express; she seemed to be making light work of her load, her safety valves momentarily lifting as she drifted past. Fitted with German-style smoke

The driver of 'Clan' 4-6-2 No 72005 *Clan Macgregor* awaits the 'right away' at Lancaster on 27 June 1963. *Ron Herbert*

deflectors and displaying a gleaming exterior, she looked quite wonderful. Paul studiously watched her effortless progress northwards towards Port Carlisle Junction, where she would take the former North British 'Waverley' route to Edinburgh. A 'Jubilee' suddenly burst on the scene, blocking his view of the departing express. The roar of brakes apparent as she rapidly reduced speed prior to entering Citadel station, No 45729 *Furious* was another cop! Great!

Paul screamed with delight – what a day it was turning out to be! He couldn't have found a better spot, and the sun had come out. Luckily his plan had worked and he still had four hours left before he met his father. If only Tubby and Philip could see him now, his excitement intensifying

with the arrival of Glasgow-based 'Royal Scot' No 46105
Cameron Highlander, another superb cop!

By midday four 'Jubilees' had passed in quick succession,
nd two more 'A3s' had been added to his growing list. Also
ogged were the numbers of another 'Clan', a 'Princess' and
wo 'Duchesses', the latter having been previously seen,
is only disappointment. Deciding to eat his large cache of
ies and sandwiches procured from the funeral reception,

he opened his bag, removed a bottle of Tizer and studied his notebook. Former LNER classes featured, including a solitary 'K3', two 'B1s', including the named *Alexander Reith Gray*, three 'A3s', two 'J39s', and 'J36' No 65321, the latter having clanked past minutes before. 'Black Fives' dominated the page, with 'Royal Scots', 'Patriots', Stanier 8Fs, Midland 4Fs, 'Crabs', 'Flying Pigs', 'Jinties' and Fairburn tanks. Apart from the two 'Clans', he had not seen any BR Standards, which was surprising; however, this immediately altered

with the arrival of 'Britannia' No 70052 *Firth of Tay* piloted by No 73079 on the down main line with a lengthy express. The 'Britannia' was throwing out plumes of thick black smoke as her fireman charged her firebox for the journey north, No 73079's driver delighting Paul by acknowledging his presence with a brief wave.

Paul was just about to tuck into another pork pie when a local lad cycled up.

The first 'Britannia' that Paul saw at Carlisle was No 70052 *Firth of Tay* seen here passing Ladies Walk sidings, Lancaster on 30 March 1964. *Roy Herbert*

'Where's your bike?' he enquired, glancing into Paul's lunchbox.

'At home, why?'

'Well, *Merlin*'s on Carlisle Canal shed and I'm off to cop er. You could have come.'

'Damn!' thought Paul, immediately suggesting that e could ride on the saddle. The lad refused and asked to look at Paul's notebook, before grunting that he had seen nothing of note. As he raised a pedal preparing to depart, aul anxiously grabbed his arm before enquiring as to other amers on Canal shed.

'There's a "D49" in store and I've copped a couple of Glens" in the past. Now it's mainly "A3s" and visiting A2s", plus the odd named "B1". Anyway, you've picked a ood spot. I often come here after school.'

He sped off, leaving behind an exasperated fellow potter. Still, it was a thoughtful act by a complete stranger. hilip had been correct – 'A4s' did visit Canal shed. How he onged to be there!

His frustration instantly vanished when 'A2' No 0536 *Trimbush* appeared with a lengthy express. What nagnificent-looking locomotives! Transfixed, Paul watched er coast towards Citadel station until she disappeared. His rst 'A2'. Wow, what a cop!

Introduced by Edward Thompson, Chief Mechanical ngineer of the LNER at the end of the Second World War, ney were powerful and impressive machines, being similar his 'A1' Class, although they had smaller driving wheels nd a higher tractive effort. They were subjected to various nodifications to improve efficiency, and five were rebuilt ith double blastpipes and multiple-valve regulators.

'Princess' No 46210 *Lady Patricia* sauntered northwards n a Birmingham to Glasgow express, quickly followed by a io of 'Black Fives', bringing him down to earth. The arrival f 'Jubilee' No 45713 *Renown* restored his spirits; however, eak' diesel D14 hardly raised any adrenalin as she purred outh. Yet another trip goods sauntered along the avoiding

'Magnificent-looking' 'A2' No 60536 *Trimbush* was Paul's first 'A2' cop, an he was impressed by her handsome lines, exemplified here by No 6053 *Bachelor's Button* at Aberdeen with a Glasgow-bound express on 7 Augus 1961. *Ray Ruffell, Silver Link Publishing collection*

lines hauled by 4F No 44008. Minutes later 'J39' No 6488 wheezed past with a local passenger, followed by Fowle tank No 42304, travelling light-engine towards Kingmoo shed. Eight minutes elapsed before Standard Class 5 N 73123 laboured through, towing English Electric Type diesel-electric D219, which had failed.

Paul suddenly glanced at his watch and froze. He ha been spotting for more than five hours and should have me his father five minutes ago. 'N2' No 69564 clattered pas on the avoiding line, and Paul hastily recorded her numbe before racing back to Bridge Street. He could see his father Morris Minor, which was now moving in his direction. Th passenger door swung open.

'You're late!' snapped his father as Paul flopped into th

'rincess' No 46210 *Lady Patricia* was another sighting at Carlisle. This
hotograph, showing off her sleek lines, was taken at Crewe Works on
2 April 1962. Unfortunately she was destined not to leave… *John Corkill*

ont seat. 'Where's your lunch box?' Blast – he had left it on
ne wall together with his pop. 'Oh, leave it, let's get home,'
aid his father angrily. It had been a lengthy meeting with

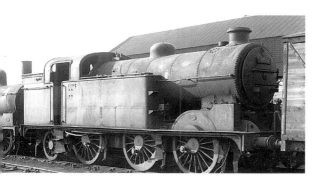

t the very end of his spotting session at Carlisle 'N2' No 69564 passed
n the avoiding line. Here she is a little later on 25 February 1962 after
ithdrawal at Eastfield shed, Glasgow, minus her coupling rods. *The late W.*
. Boyden, courtesy of Frank Hornby

the solicitor, who had gone through all the complexities of legacies, taxes and so on. Mentally tired, Mr Carr longed for his bed. As for enjoying his son's company, Paul had not taken his eyes off his notebook since departure.

'Well, did you increase your tally?' Paul beamed. 'Don't tell me. I don't want to know.'

Paul once more studied his cops, and got out his sheet book. He couldn't wait to get home and show his book to Tubby, Philip and Badger.

The day's excitement began to take its toll, and he began to doze. Mr Carr glanced at his sleeping passenger and sighed – what a head worker! The dog would have been better company – at least Buster appreciated the scenery, and barked at the sheep. He changed to a lower gear. They had reached Shap, and with luck would be home before dusk.

7
PRESTON

Philip watched with growing apprehension as the 'Caledonian' rounded the curve, at an astonishing speed. No 46232 *Duchess of Montrose* suddenly lurched and leapt off the track, crashing into 'Standard 4' tank No 80054 waiting in the loop.

'You were going too fast!' cried Philip as he picked up the Duchess', checking for damage. Paul grimaced and glanced out of the window. It was still pouring down, thwarting any attempts to trainspot. This had prompted a spell of experimenting with various layouts in the spare bedroom, and vast quantities of Hornby Dublo three-rail track lay spread over the carpet.

'We should have used large-radius curves,' Paul muttered as Philip re-railed the undamaged 'Pacific'.

'You still drive like a madman. Just as well it's not a real steam engine otherwise the train would soon be on the floor. Take it easy with the controller, will you?'

Having been duly chastised, Paul resumed control and this time the 'Duchess' successfully cleared the curve. Seconds later Stanier 8F No 48158 trundled past with a coal train, and Paul switched off the power and sat back.

'Cracked it!' he yelled.

Glancing out of the window, he noticed that the rain had eased, and he began to grow restless.

'Phil, it's Friday tomorrow – let's go to Liverpool Exchange and see what "Clan" brings in the 7.17 Perth.'

'Might be a "Jub",' replied Philip, 'although it's a "Clan" most Friday nights.'

'We could ask Tubby, Badger and Pearson,' added Paul, rubbing his hands in anticipation, his boredom having vanished together with the rain!

Tubby was fiddling with one of the station's chocolate dispensers. Having duly placed his money in the slot, it seemed reluctant to part with a bar of Nestles chocolate. He tugged again and earned his reward. Pearson was also occupied, punching his name on a strip of metal, utilising one of the numerous platform machines to be found on this former Lancashire & Yorkshire terminus, the old company still intent on parting its customers from their remaining coppers.

Electric multiple units bustled to and fro with suburban

Liverpool Exchange station on 13 March 1966. 'Black Five' 4-6-0 No 45260 is at the head of the 16.40 service to Glasgow and Edinburgh. *The late J. M. Tolson, courtesy of Frank Hornby*

services to Southport and the suburbs. Having spotted electric parcels van No M28497M, Philip was about to set off down the platform to examine it.

'Come on, Phil, never mind the parcels van!' cried Paul. 'There's a former Lancashire & Yorkshire Railway radial tank on pilot duty.'

One of the last survivors of a once numerous class, No 50721 panted restlessly at the end of the platform, her friendly young fireman inviting them on board. The cab seemed quite spacious, and Philip enquired as to the driver's whereabouts. 'Oh, he's just gone to the pub. He'll be back in about half an hour, then it's my turn,' the fireman chirped, rubbing his hands with glee. He quite liked the old engine, as she was easy to fire and steamed well. They chatted for some considerable time before departing, having been encouraged to place a few rounds into the firebox.

A couple of 'Black Fives' provided limited entertainment, but the Perth was now overdue, and they waited anxiously for the anticipated 'Clan'. After a lengthy delay, No 72001 *Clan Cameron* coasted in with the heavy express, Paul

Ex-L&YR 2-4-2 radial tank No 50721 on pilot duty at Liverpool Exchange in August 1960. *Ron Coffey*

ecstatically whooping as she gently rolled to a halt. Suddenly her safety valves lifted and with a deafening roar a plume of steam shot towards the station roof.

'She's got an enthusiastic fireman! Fancy blowing off at the end of the journey – what a waste of coal and effort!' shouted Philip.

'Well, she was running late, so you would expect a response from the crew,' Paul retorted. Philip didn't really rate 'Clans'; Paul on the other hand quite liked them and managed to gain the driver's attention.

'Are these good engines?' he shouted.

'Depends which one you get. They're all right on certain jobs, like a fitted goods.' The driver turned away and lit a cigarette, effectively ending the conversation. Trainspotters often stretched his patience after a long and tedious day. Personally, he couldn't care less whether he had a 'Clan' or a 'Jubilee', just as long as they rode well and steamed!

No 50721 puffed out with the empty stock, allowing the 'Clan' to proceed to Bank Hall shed. Things went a little flat after her departure, so the boys decided to return home via Lime Street station. As they sauntered towards the entrance Paul took time to study the train departure board.

'Listen, why don't we have a day at Preston? We can see all the West Coast traffic as well as the Blackpool excursions. We can go from here via Ormskirk, or via Wigan if we go from Lime Street.'

'Let's go from here for a change,' said Tubby. 'When we go, can my cousin come?' he continued.

'Don't see why not,' Paul replied.

'It's just that he's a bus and diesel fanatic,' Tubby added cautiously.

'Doesn't matter,' chirped Philip as Paul pulled a face. 'The more the merrier.'

'Good – I'll tell him to bring some sandwiches,' beamed Tubby.

The following Saturday Tubby introduced his cousin Andrew to the group. Paul gaped. Andy was so thin he could slide through a keyhole, and would have had no difficulty entering any firebox door. 'Blimey, you look like Laurel and Hardy!' he quipped, bringing chuckles from his pals. 'Come on, let's go to Exchange. Hopefully we'll have a good day.'

'And see lots of diesels,' added Andy cheerfully, much to Paul's annoyance.

Apart from Andy, most of the group were leaning out of carriage windows as they passed Bank Hall shed, observing un-named 'Patriot' No 45517, Standard Class 2 No 78043 and former L&YR 'Pugs' Nos 51206 and 51237. However, their journey soon became mundane, with virtually no sightings until they joined the West Coast Main Line.

'"Semi"!' screamed Badger. Whoosh – No 46242 *City of Glasgow* tore past, rattling the windows, as they desperately

he former L&YR Bank Hall shed seen from the road bridge in about 960. In the foreground is 'Black Five' No 44767. *Ron Coffey*

Ex-L&YR 0-4-0 'Pugs' Nos 51204 and 51237 were glimpsed as the boys passed Bank Hall shed. Here is the second of the pair, photographed many years earlier at Bank Hall on 1 June 1948. *Frank Hornby*

In June 1961 unnamed 'Patriot' No 45547 threads her way through the former CLC Skelton Junction with an express freight. Fifty-two of these useful locomotives were constructed by the LMS during the early 1930s many being rebuilt with taper boilers during the Stanier era. Ten of the unrebuilt engines remained nameless, much to the chagrin of spotters It is poignant that a new 'Patriot' is currently being constructed at the Llangollen Railway; numbered 45552, she will carry the name *The Unknown Warrior*, a fitting memorial to those killed in conflict. *The late David Frost Collection courtesy of the GWS, Didcot*

tucked back into the corridor, enveloped in smoke. Pearson swore – they had seen her before.

'Wow, that was close!' grinned Paul, returning to his former position.

'No 46242 *City of Glasgow* tore past, rattling the windows.' Here she does something similar at Lancaster station on 5 June 1962. *Ron Herbert*

They arrived at Preston on time, having passed 'Jubilee' No 45629 *Straits Settlements* and a solitary 'WD'. After congratulating the crew of BR Standard No 75046 on their prompt arrival, they jostled towards an incoming express. 'Laurel and Hardy' swapped sandwiches as they struggled to keep up.

Stanier 'Black Five' No 44686 clanked past, before grinding to a halt alongside a small group of young spotters.

Preston station on 20 June 1964. 'Crab' 2-6-0 No 42932 leaves with the 4.25pm train from Manchester Victoria to Blackpool. *The late J. M. Tolson, courtesy of Frank Hornby*

A 'Jubilee' at Preston. This is No 45694 *Bellerophon* south of the station photographed from the 09.25 Crewe-Perth express on 19 June 1965. *Ray Ruffell, Silver Link Publishing collection*

'Not very exciting,' blurted Badger, clearly unimpressed.

'Actually she's one of a pair built in 1951. My Dad says that they are both excellent engines. He rates them the equal of a good "Jubilee".' There was no stopping Philip now, and he started describing the benefits of roller bearings and the advantages of a double chimney, mesmerising the group of local lads gathered around the cab. Paul was watching for any further sign of movement, having just spotted 'Jinty' No 47360 lurking behind some parcels vans.

Shortly after the departure of the 'Black Five', 'Jubilee' No 45556 *Nova Scotia* steamed through hauling empty stock; unfortunately she proved to be a notorious 'stink', and was greeted accordingly. Things improved when 'Royal Scot' No 46104 *Scottish Borderer* pulled in with a relief. Shouts of joy echoed down the platform – a cop at last, and an excellent one at that! More 'Black Fives' arrived, many

'Black Five' 4-6-0s Nos 44686 and 44687 were built in 1951 with Caprotti valve gear, Skefco roller bearings and a double chimney, as seen in this portrait of the first of the pair at Preston on 12 June 1964. *Ron Herbert*

on freights, together with a couple of 'Crabs' and Stanier 8Fs. But where were the namers? The arrival of an unrebuilt 'Patriot' brought a fresh surge of excitement, only to be revealed as un-named No 45542. Badger could not believe it. Un-named 'Patriots' were not exactly common, and to see two in succession was unusual to say the least.

'Talking of "Patriots", my Dad says that Edge Hill's rebuilt "Patriot" *Sir Herbert Walker K.C.B.* is one of the star performers,' voiced Philip.

'She's a ruddy stink!' bleated Paul. 'I've seen her loads of times.'

Andy suddenly let out an excited cry, as Sulzer Bo-Bo No D5015 motored in with a train from Crewe. He raced off running alongside the locomotive as she purred to a halt. 'Now that's what I call an efficient locomotive!' he shouted, rapidly explaining how diesels had revolutionised American railways. 'They're far more reliable and powerful than any steam engine,' he prattled, angering Paul.

'Is that so? Well, how come they're always breaking down?'

Andy hesitated. 'I suppose drivers are still not familiar with how they work – after all, there are so many different types.'

'Well, they're hardly standard or simple machines. With a steam engine you can generally overcome problems – with a diesel you just grind to a halt,' Paul scornfully remarked. He was about to say more when Andy wisely announced that he was leaving the station for a couple of hours to go bus-spotting. As he wandered off, Paul turned to Tubby asking, 'How long before he goes home to Lichfield?'

'In two days time,' frowned his pal.

'He wants to stay there,' Paul replied tartly.

The next hour provided two surprises. Former LNER 'K3' No 61853 steamed through with a twelve-coach Blackpool excursion. Ten minutes later 'Peak' diesel No D2 *Helvellyn* arrived light-engine, travelling northwards, astounding Philip. These diesels were fairly rare – English lectric Type 4s were much more plentiful. Paul grinned, elighted that Andy had missed her.

'Princess' 'Pacific' No 46209 *Princess Beatrice* appeared n a Scottish relief, Tubby and Pearson gratefully jotting own her number.

Apart from the normal collection of 'Black Fives' and tandards, their venue had not provided a great many cops.

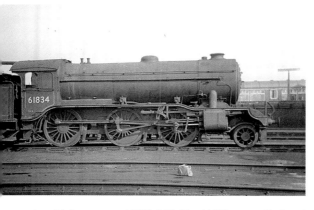

surprise sighting was ex-LNER 'K3' No 61853 on a Blackpool xcursion. Found all over the former LNER system, another member of is Gresley-designed class is seen many miles south at Cambridge on 7 eptember 1961. *Ray Ruffell, Silver Link Publishing collection*

heir luck improved when 'Duchess' No 46222 *Queen Mary* rifted through with the 'Caledonian' express to a chorus f cheers, most copping this elusive engine. Sixteen minutes iter 'Duchess' No 46241 *City of Edinburgh* coasted to a alt amid a chorus of boos – she was hardly rare. The 'Lakes xpress' saw the arrival of 'Royal Scot' No 46146 *The Rifle rigade*, and shortly after her departure 'Jubilee' Nos 45567 *outh Australia* and 45571 *South Africa* steamed through

with fitted freights. Then there was a short lull before 4
No 44550 wheezed to a halt at a water column with a ten
coach Blackpool special. Passengers leaned out of windows
enquiring as to their impromptu halt. The 4F appeared to b
short of steam and the driver quickly turned on the blowe
while the fireman shovelled coal forward. Six minutes late
they were off, to a barrage of abuse. They were late!

The authorisation by the LMS to construct 497 4Fs u
to the Second World War is puzzling. Apart from Derby
built examples, most footplate crews had little affection fo
the class, finding them temperamental and difficult to fire
especially on passenger duties. It is significant that forme
Cheshire Lines footplate crews often preferred a 'J11' t

Stanier's 'Coronation' 'Pacifics' were the stars of the West Coast Mai
Line. Here is *Coronation* herself, No 46220, her Carlisle crew awaiting 'righ
away' at Euston before leaving with the 10.35am express for Carlisle o
30 June 1961. *Ray Ruffell, Silver Link Publishing collection*

he friends were pleased to see 'Coronation' No 46222 *Queen Mary* on
e 'Caledonian' express. The power of these 'Pacifics' is demonstrated
y the same locomotive departing from Lancaster on 13 February 1962.
on Herbert

number of the locomotives were named after cities served by the LMS.
ere is No 46237 *City of Bristol* at Perth, heading the 12.20pm express to
uston on 17 August 1961. *Ray Ruffell, Silver Link Publishing collection*

The arrival of oft-seen No 46241 *City of Edinburgh* was greeted by a chorus of boos. Sadly, not many years later she became the last Stanier 'Pacific' at Edge Hill shed, and is seen here waiting to be towed away for scrapping on 27 November 1964. *John Corkill*

a 4F, bearing in mind that the former were introduced in 1901. Surely the LMS-designed Hughes-Fowler 'Crab' was far superior?

Philip suggested that they visit Preston engine shed after lunch. Its roof had burned down the previous year, and it was now quite dilapidated. They all agreed, apart from Tubby, who decided to wait for Andy, his cousin having promised to bring him some Cornish pasties on his return.

'Blimey, Tubby, what have you done with your sandwiches?' asked Paul.

'Eaten them most probably,' sneered Pearson.

'No I haven't – I gave most of them to Andy. He only brought a couple.'

'Well, he must have gone by bus to Cornwall for them. He should be back by now. If he's not back soon, we will just have to go without him,' Paul growled.

While they were eating, Andy returned, jubilant that he

Nearly 500 LMS 4F 0-6-0s were built, but they were generally unpopular with crews, who found them temperamental and difficult to fire. No 44464 was photographed at Carlisle Kingmoor shed on 30 May 1963. *John Corkill*

had seen an old pre-war Lytham St Annes Leyland Titan double-decker bus on a school outing. In his excitement he had forgotten to bring Tubby his pasties, so Tubby angrily blurted that he had missed D2 *Helvellyn*, beating Paul to the punch.

'Saw her at Derby last year,' said Andy, as Tubby stormed off to the station cafeteria. Paul silently cursed. Andy was beginning to get on his nerves.

It was not far to the shed, the odd spot of rain encouraging an increase in pace as they rapidly made their way through the side streets.

'It's around the bend,' voiced Philip.

'Just like us,' muttered Badger, as more drops of rain splattered on the pavement.

They ran the rest of the way, leaving Tubby in their wake, and found shelter in the shed's doorway. By the time Tubby arrived it was raining fairly heavily, and he tried to push his way into the group. There was barely room as it was, and Tubby swore as rain trickled down his neck from a broken gutter.

'Shove up!' he moaned.

'There's no room – you'll have to find somewhere else!' shouted Pearson angrily. Tubby charged forward and pressed even harder, crushing his duffle bag and his pals.

'It's ironic – here we are trying to shelter from the rain in a shed that's got no roof,' blurted Paul, suddenly seeing the funny side of their dilemma. They all laughed – it really was a bit rich!

The rain soon stopped and they emerged to view a dismal spectacle, the shed apparently devoid of life. A couple of

The boys found Preston's shed apparently devoid of life. The roofless building is seen on 10 November 1962, after it had closed. 'Patriot' No 45543 *Home Guard* is stored, among a variety of other locomotives. *The late J. M. Tolson, courtesy of Frank Hornby*

oads were packed with withdrawn 'Super Ds' and a solitary
.&YR 0-6-0 saddle tank. 'Kitson Dock Tank' No 47009
nd Stanier Class 4 tank No 42638 clanked slowly past as
adger jotted down the numbers of the withdrawn engines.

'Just imagine preparing a loco in the pouring rain on a
ice cold January morning,' said Philip. 'It must have been a
ightmare.'

Bitterly disappointed, they stood silently amid the pools
f oily water, soot and ash surrounding the empty pits. It

couple of roads at Preston shed were packed with withdrawn 'Super Ds',
sight to sadden any spotter. More of the redundant 0-8-0s stretch away
infinity at the former LNWR siding at Wharton, Winsford, Cheshire, on
3 March 1959. The author has spoken to drivers about these engines, and
any held them in high esteem, despite their antiquated appearance. They
uld certain pull and generally kept going, even when short of steam. Their
artime contribution was immense as they handled a vast proportion of
eight on the former LNWR tracks during the last conflict. The author
dmits to having a soft spot for these wonderful wheezing machines. *The
te David Frost Collection, courtesy of the GWS, Didcot*

was hardly the highlight they had expected, so they plodded back to Preston station to find Andy, who had fortuitously declined their invitation.

They arrived to find him standing alongside Metro Vickers Co-Bo diesel No D5710 on a late-running Barrow train piloted by 'Black Five' No 45189, the Co-Bo having failed at Crewe. Paul was ecstatic, Andy bearing the brunt of a few choice remarks. However, he appeared to take the ribbing in good grace, although he was secretly seething, and was more than glad when the train departed. Moments later 'Britannia' No 70051 *Firth of Forth* sauntered through with a southbound parcels train, increasing Paul's good humour. Another good cop! He was beginning to enjoy himself!

Their day was quickly drawing to a close so, feeling a little tired, they reluctantly boarded a local train back to

Back at the station 'Britannia' No 70051 *Firth of Forth* provided another good cop for Paul. Here she is at Grange-over-Sands arriving with the 14.23 service to Euston on 2 December 1966. *Ray Ruffell, Silver Link Publishing collection*

Liverpool Exchange. Tubby flopped into a vacant seat, and felt his blazer. It was still damp and he was just about to gripe when 9F No 92017 steamed past. He jumped up, and Pearson and Paul dashed into the corridor to get a closer look. Tubby reached inside his duffle bag for his *ABC Combined* and froze – his hand was sticky as he extracted his prize possession. He gazed in horror at the cover depicting 'Duchess' 'Pacific' *City of Liverpool*, its crimson livery having changed to purple, blackcurrant and apple clinging to the book's outer pages. Trembling, he tried opening the sticky pages, ruefully contemplating his decision to save two Lyons fruit pies for the journey home, and his bullish attempts while seeking shelter at Preston shed.

'Go to the toilet and wipe it with some toilet paper,' said Andy sympathetically, watching his pal.

'Don't use water!' cried Philip, getting in on the act, 'otherwise you'll ruin it.'

A few minutes later the corridor door slowly opened and Paul studied Tubby with growing concern, after being informed of his dilemma. He had never seen him so despondent – he could barely speak.

'Well, Tubby, how's the book now?' asked Philip tentatively.

Tubby held it up, only to have it snatched by Paul. After carefully inspection, he handed it back.

'Tubby, the *Combined* has had it. You'll just have to buy another one, and transfer all the numbers.'

'Yeah, that should take you all of five minutes,' said Pearson contemptuously. Paul stared angrily at him – sometimes he could be a right pain.

'But most of the pages are stuck together,' Tubby moaned. 'If I try to separate them, they'll tear, and I will lose the numbers.'

'Not if you use a razor blade,' said Badger. 'You can then peel them apart. Anyway, I'll help you,' he added, trying to cheer him up. Tubby smiled and shrugged, and looked out of the window for the remainder of the journey, uncharacteristically staying in his seat on passing Bank Hall shed.

After a brief spell at Liverpool Lime Street station, they boarded a local train to Mossley Hill, Paul carefully underlining his named cops in his *ABC*. After wearily trudging up the ramp, they said their farewells, Paul informing Andy that he could join them on any future trip, buoyed by the thought of taking the mickey.

Tubby and Andy plodded home. 'I'll never go with that lot again,' complained Andy. 'That Paul really gets up my nose.'

Not that Tubby cared. He was having a bad day, and his world had fallen apart.

8
MANCHESTER, LEEDS AND YORK

The room temperature was rising rapidly. 'Look, son, if you're determined to an engine driver, then go and see John Franklin at number twelve – he'll put you wise. Never mind what Philip says – find out for yourself. Go and see him.'

Determination echoed in Mr Carr's voice – somehow he had to rid Paul of his pipe dream. He felt that railway employment only offered a limited future; of course, he could be wrong but, thinking of Joe, he intensified his efforts.

'Look, what have you got to lose, eh? Nothing. Go and see the man – you may find his advice useful.'

Five minutes later Mrs Franklin opened the door to be greeted by an apprehensive Paul, his father having won the day.

'Excuse me, Mrs Franklin, is your husband in?'

'Aye, lad, he is. You're Mrs Carr's boy, aren't you? Paul isn't it? Wait in the parlour – he'll not be a minute.'

Paul sat down, noticing that the room was quite ordinary - pictures of holidays spent at Morecambe adorned the hearth – but it had a warm and friendly atmosphere and he was soon at ease. Quietly the door opened and Mr John Franklin entered. He had still to achieve top link status, having joined the LMS railway as a cleaner, his ambitions confined to driving shunting locomotives after years firing the various classes allocated to Edge Hill shed. Having exchanged greetings, Paul speedily explained the reason for his unexpected call.

'It was my father's idea,' he gushed. 'He thinks I shouldn't go on the railway without talking to you. I want to be a driver, you see, but...' Paul hesitated. 'Well, my father thinks there's no real future in it.'

'I see – so you want to be a driver?' Mr Franklin half smiled and slowly lit his pipe, then stared steadily into the fire. 'Ambitious are you?' Paul's head nodded vigorously 'Thought so – then don't go on the railway. Promotion's too slow. Join the RAF like your brother – better future all round for a bright lad like you.'

'But I thought all drivers loved their jobs.'

'Well, that depends. Don't think engine-driving is always a pleasure. It can be damn frustrating at times. We all have our off days you know. Don't get me wrong, I'm not condemning it – it's provided me with a reasonable living all these years. I've had some good mates, and I've lost a few…' His voice trailed off, tinged with sadness, or was it bitterness, Paul wondered.

His thoughts were interrupted by Mrs Franklin, who breezed in with two steaming cups of tea. That interlude over Mr Franklin methodically puffed his pipe and continued.

'Things are changing rapidly at present. They'll no need as many drivers as before, what with diesels and such Fancy being a cleaner for a few years – shovelling five tons of coal, getting up at four in the morning or emptying a smokebox on a nice windy day?' he chuckled, as if enjoying some private joke. 'That'll knock some of the romance out of you.'

He studied Paul's face keenly, knowing he'd been hard on the lad. Still, it was for his own good. Too many youngsters joined the railway with their heads in the clouds only to leave within a few years, disillusioned with pay and prospects. Mind you, the lad looked determined enough Perhaps he would make it – aye, perhaps he would.

Paul stood up, his thoughts confused. Obviously some drivers were not content with their lot. The spell had been broken and his world would never be quite the same again.

'Well, son, how did it go?' Mr Carr stared at Paul curiously.

'Oh, all right Dad,' he replied bluntly. 'Must go now – I've got to meet Philip.'

Paul left the room like a scalded cat, Mr Carr's eyes following him. He was lying, and they both knew it, so perhaps some good would come of the meeting after all, although he doubted if anything could put Paul off joining the railway. He shrugged – why on earth couldn't Paul come and work with him at Cammell Laird's shipyard? He could easily get him a good job. Now there was a place with a future, but no, Paul remained defiant. Kids, he muttered – why were they always a problem?

'Here, this is the page.' Paul stared at Philip's maths book and quickly copied the answers to the previous night's homework.

'Thanks, Phil – better get a few wrong or it'll look obvious.' Seconds later, he sat back smiling. 'Phil, did you do that poem on your favourite hobby for old Barlow? You know, the one he set us last week?'

'Yes.'

Paul looked at his pal. 'Mine's on spotting.'

Philip grinned. 'Original, aren't you? I would never have guessed! Incidentally, talking of spotting, I'm thinking of going to York in a fortnight's time. Are you coming?'

'I can't afford it,' Paul replied.

'Not to worry. I'll lend you a couple of pounds – you can pay me back later.'

His pal's face brightened. 'That's good of you, Phil. Yes, I'd like to go, although I'd set my heart on Doncaster.' He paused. 'By the way, my Dad sent me round to see Mr Franklin yesterday.'

'The Edge Hill driver?' interrupted Philip. 'My Dad knows him.'

'Yes, anyway he didn't exactly encourage me to take up driving. He reckons promotion's too slow.'

Philip looked thoughtful. 'My Dad says that too, but he still made it. Could be sour grapes. I wouldn't let it put me off.'

'It didn't,' retorted Paul, angry that his friend should

even think such a thing.

Tubby's frame suddenly blocked out the daylight – for a big lad he was remarkably quiet on his feet. 'Plotting another trip?' he asked inquisitively.

'Nosey, aren't you?' Paul said tartly, his pride still smarting.

Philip smiled. 'As a matter of fact, we're thinking of going to York. Do you want to come?'

'Yes, when are you going?'

'Fortnight on Saturday,' replied Philip, glancing at Paul for approval. 'We'll catch the nine o'clock to Newcastle.'

'Anyone else going – I mean, besides us?' Tubby enquired.

Paul looked up. 'I shouldn't think so – everyone's broke.'

Even on a Saturday Liverpool Lime Street station teemed and bustled with life, people scurrying and weaving towards unknown goals, a human whirlpool caught in the morning rush hour. Tubby, Paul and Philip battled towards the ticket barrier, happy moles in this gloomy world. Philip glanced towards the station clock – 8.45am, fifteen minutes to go before the Newcastle's departure.

Once past the barrier Tubby surged ahead, clearing a path through the busy concourse. I mustn't lose my identity card, Philip mused. He tightened his grip – clutching the card brought a sense of comfort, and at least he wouldn't have to pay full fare. On reaching the booking office window his companions briskly purchased their day returns – now it was his turn.

'Privilege return to York, please.' Philip handed in his written request form and showed his identity card, grateful for the travel concessions given to the dependants of railwaymen.

'Change at Leeds,' came the mumbled reply.

Picking up his ticket, Philip rejoined his pals only to hear Paul voicing a complaint. 'It's a cheek charging us adult fare – after all, we're still at school.' Philip looked away embarrassed. Once aged fourteen, juveniles were classed as adults – an injustice perhaps, but a rule the railway seemed reluctant to change.

The boys ran up the departure platform. Tubby, struggling to keep up, ground to a halt, completely puffed. His pals raced on, excitedly pointing to the front on the train, their delight obvious – *two* engines rested there. Gosh! A double-header! Tubby lumbered after them, slowly closing the distance. Looks like a 'Mickey' and a 'Scot', he contemplated as his companions reached the engines.

'Come on, Tubby!' they shouted, gesticulating for more effort. Paul thought Tubby looked like a charging bull elephant as he covered the last few yards. He immediately collapsed onto a convenient platform trolley, and wrote down the engine numbers.

'Royal Scot' No 46109 *Royal Engineer* nestled behind No 45250, a grubby 'Black Five'. The paintwork of the 'Scot' looked splendid, like a dog in good condition, her coat gleaming. Philip examined her shed plate and returned with a puzzled expression.

'Thought so – she's a Leeds Holbeck engine. I think she's just come out of Crewe Works. What a smashing cop for you both.'

His pals beamed with delight – this engine was rarely seen in Liverpool. The 'Black Five' looked insignificant compared with her partner; however, sometimes appearances are deceiving, and this was such an occasion.

The rebuilt 'Royal Scots' held the distinction of being one of the finest 4-6-0s ever to run on British metals, taking nothing away from the Great Western's 'Castle' Class. Equally, the 'Black Fives' were in a league of their own, ubiquitous, versatile and free-running, they formed the backbone of the London Midland Region's motive power.

Seconds passed until the shrill sound of an inspector's whistle sent the boys scurrying aboard. A minute later they were climbing the stiff gradient leading to Edge Hill, the uncoordinated exhaust of the two locomotives thrilling and memorable. Once clear of Huyton the engines really showed their pace and the delights of the English countryside danced before absorbent eyes. BR Standard No 76079* stormed past with some parcels vans seconds before their passage through Salford. Within minutes the train was screeching to a halt, a signal check heralding their arrival at Manchester Exchange and Victoria.

On reaching the combined stations the boys immediately spotted a former LMS 4-4-0 on banking duties. Philip called out her number. '40671! That's all they're fit for, or piloting She couldn't pull a sausage. The Southern "L1s" are much better engines.'

Paul frowned. Now where had he heard that before? Ignoring the remark, he carefully studied the locomotive. Her driving wheels seemed enormously large – approximately 7 feet in diameter – giving an impression of power, however misleadingly.

Sparks filled the air as the engines stormed up the steep

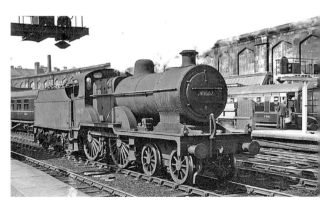

Philip considered that the ex-LMS 2P 4-4-0s were only fit for banking or pilot duties. No 40657 stands on one of the middle roads at Carlisle Citadel station on 16 June 1958, possibly acting as station pilot. *Frank Hornby*

ank to Miles Platting with grateful assistance. The endless
suburbs eventually faded and they drifted into Stalybridge
station. Philip pointed to a public bar located on the
platform, but Paul's suggestion that they go for a pint was
lost on Tubby. After jotting down the numbers of a 'WD'
and a Stanier tank, they resumed their journey. The engines
were now climbing steadily, their exhaust noticeably sharper
as they laboured over the Pennines, the bleak countryside a
sharp contrast to that previously seen.

A whistle shrieked and they plunged into Standedge
tunnel, and the carriage lights blinked twice before flickering
on. Eerie shadows flickered along the corridor, darting and
snatching at them in constant waves. Tubby shifted uneasily,
nearly deafened by the roar of the train.

'How long is this?' he shouted apprehensively.

'Over three miles,' answered Philip.

'Blimey!'

Paul glanced at the window, noticing what appeared to
be rain against the pane. It couldn't be – he blinked and
stared into the gloom. Tapping Philip, he motioned towards
the glass. 'Looks like rain, but it can't be, not inside a tunnel.'

'You're dead right – we're taking on water. There are
troughs in here – it's one of the few level stretches on the
line.'

'Rubbish!' Paul exclaimed. 'They don't have troughs in
tunnels – even Tubby knows that.'

Tubby looked on helplessly. Paul grabbed the window
strap and released it, but immediately spray and smoke
forced its rapid return. He coughed and spluttered before
nodding at Philip. 'You know, you may be right at that!' His
pal normally was, and it niggled him.

A prodigious number of filthy 'WD' 'Austerity' freight
locomotives plied the Huddersfield area, together with
the odd Fowler Class 4 tank. In the town's elegant, early
Victorian station, unrebuilt 'Patriot' No 45505 *The Royal
Army Ordnance Corps* waited at signals on a westbound
parcels. Her fireman stared intently at the starter signal as if
his life depended on its early release. Eventually it came off,

'A prodigious number of filthy "WD" "Austerity" freight locomotives plied the Huddersfield area.' These wartime workhorses were certainly not glamorous. After the war 200 of the 2-8-0 design were purchased by the LNER from the Ministry of Supply, then in 1948 British Railways bought 533 more, together with 25 2-10-0s. A pair of 2-8-0s are seen here, No 90201 at Crewe Works on 8 April 1962 and No 90271 at Carnforth on 3 December 1966. *Frank Hornby/Ray Ruffell, Silver Link Publishing collection*

nd the train snorted off towards Springwood Junction.

Their own train laboured on, railway lines popping up ontinuously, providing few trainspotting opportunities apart from a momentary glimpse of an ex-LNER Class O4' at Ravensthorpe. Batley passed, then Morley Tunnel, omewhat shorter than its predecessor, much to Tubby's elief. Emerging into mist and drizzle, they drifted downhill owards Farnley and Holbeck sheds, increasing their drenalin. Tubby's excited cry alerted them to the presence

Jnrebuilt 'Patriot' No 45505 *The Royal Army Ordnance Corps* was spotted t Huddersfield station. The locomotive is seen her at Lancaster Green yre on 11 May 1962. *Ron Herbert*

f 'Jubilee' No 45581 *Bihar and Orissa* and Ivatt 'Flying Pig' No 43038.

Carriage lights again pierced the gloom, the drizzle aving turned to heavy rain, producing a steady stream of roplets that cascaded down the carriage window, marring he view. Philip frantically wiped away the condensation, aware that they were running over the series of arches approaching Holbeck shed. Minutes earlier they had passed Farnley Junction and shed, recording 'WD' Nos 90407 and 90728, Stanier 8F No 48055 and 'B1' No 61218. Paul opened a carriage window, braving the downpour, while Tubby positioned himself at a convenient window at the end of the corridor.

'Holbeck shed's coming up!' shouted Philip, frantically rewiping the window. The rain suddenly eased, and they gazed towards the shed. Rows of engines stood enticingly but due to the angle of the roundhouse sidings their numbers were either too far away for identification, or masked.

'Looks like a "Scot". Damn, I can't make out her number.'

'"Brit"!' screamed Philip, leaning over Paul's shoulder and spotting the engine coasting tender-first under the viaduct towards Leeds city station. '70044 *Earl Haig*. Look an ex-works "Jub"! Four fifty-five sixty-four, *New South Wales*! Brilliant! Two new namers!'

An unidentifiable 'A3' 'Pacific' simmered outside one of the roundhouses, bringing groans of exasperation. Seconds later they had passed the shed, disappointed with the results having observed at least three 'Jubilees'. A lengthy signal check outside Leeds City station put paid to plans for a flying visit to Leeds Central station. Chattering excitedly they tumbled onto the platform, Tubby's insistence that the number of the elusive 'Royal Scot' ended in thirteen exasperating Paul. How could he be so sure? He remained unconvinced. Philip also had doubts. Not that it mattered – he had copped the entire class.

York at last! Paul could scarcely believe it, the thrill of dashing up the East Coast Main Line still flowing in his veins. They had overtaken a 'K3' on the way, romping along with an unfitted freight. What a sight she'd made! He shut his eyes and mentally recaptured her throwing up columns of sooty smoke from her enormous boiler. With a smile he recalled their furious dash at Leeds for the connection to

York, Tubby having clumsily dropped his sandwich box, causing a minor panic.

Their diesel railcar slowly negotiated the last few yards before grinding to a halt underneath York station's magnificent roof. Its splendour passed unnoticed, however, their gaze firmly fixed on 'A3' 'Pacific' No 60055 *Woolwinder* waiting in the opposite platform with a heavy King's Cross express. Spotters flocked around the engine, trying unsuccessfully to engage the crew in conversation. Paul quickly joined them after surging ahead of his pals.

As the boys approached York they overtook a 'K3' with an unfitted freight, remarking on the massive boilers carried by these engines. 'K3' No 61963 heads a fitted freight towards London through Stratford (ER) on 27 February 1960. *Frank Hornby*

Woolwinder simmered quietly, wisps of steam escaping from her gleaming cylinders, radiating a pleasant warmth. A jet of light grey smoke snaked from her chimney towards the cavernous roof, which reverberated with the sound of slamming carriage doors, signifying the train's imminent departure. Paul took a deep breath, intoxicated by the warm

'This is York.' On 15 July 1961 a group of spotters have congregated at the north end of the station to watch the comings and goings, including 'B16' 4-6-0 No 61455. *John Corkill*

aroma of oil and steam. Touching the engine's nameplate, his fingers received a film of dirt and oil, instantly removed by wiping them on his new grey trousers as he reflected on his previous 'A3' sightings at Carlisle.

Philip and Tubby finally arrived and began examining the engine. 'She's a real beauty – even my Dad says these double-chimney versions are excellent steamers.'

What – Philip praising an ex-LNER engine? Paul could hardly believe his ears. He gave his pal a provocative look. 'How does your Dad know? He doesn't drive them.'

'Don't be stupid, Paul – how do you think he knows?' Paul shut up.

This 'Pacific' belonged to the same class as the world-famous *Flying Scotsman* locomotive. Introduced as Class 'A1' in 1922, they handled the bulk of the Anglo-Scottish expresses, being free-running and reliable. Later they were modified to improve their steaming, becoming Class 'A3'. With the recent addition of double blastpipe and chimney,

Surprisingly, Philip pronounced 'A3' 'Pacific' No 60055 *Woolwinder* 'a real beauty'. She was photographed at King's Cross in about 1952, before the double chimney was fitted. *A. J. Pike OBE, courtesy of Frank Hornby*

they were now at their peak, but dieselisation was sealing their fate. Some of the class were still being fitted with German-type smoke deflectors, an innovation that improved a long-standing problem – a strange state of affairs when one considers that the class were shortly to be taken out of service.

Making a supreme effort to capture *Woolwinder*'s audience, No 68736, York's busy station pilot, crept quietly into view. Recently painted in former North Eastern Railway green livery, and carrying that company's coat of arms, she looked a real picture. Footsteps receded from the aristocratic 'A3' – a new star had stolen the show. On reaching her, Philip gave an impromptu speech.

The soft exhaust of the 'A3s' meant that smoke drifted down and obscured the driver's view. Experimental German-type smoke deflectors were fitted to some examples, including No 60065 *Knight of Thistle* seen here from a passing train near Peterborough. *Ray Ruffell, Silver Link Publishing collection*

'Do you know that these engines have a unique record of being built under three ownerships? First they were constructed by the North Eastern Railway, then by the London & North Eastern Railway and finally by British Railways, all to the original 1898 design, which speaks volumes for Wilson Worsdell, their designer. Oh, by the way, she's a "J72" tank.'

'We know,' smirked Tubby. 'It's written on the buffer beam.'

BR Standard Class 3 2-6-0 No 77012 passed through on her way to the shed, delighting the trio. Allocated to Scottish and North Eastern sheds, these locos were extremely elusive – York shed had a small allocation. Even Philip beamed pleased with his latest cop.

Woolwinder made a noisy departure, slipping on the

York shed had a small allocation of the very elusive BR Standard Class 3 2-6-0s, which were exclusive to Scottish and North Eastern sheds. Later they migrated south – No 77014 was photographed between Wokingham and Crowthorne in January 1967. *Ray Ruffell, Silver Link Publishing collection*

greasy rails, before barking out of the station, her exhaust deafening. Tubby counted the packed carriages. 'Fourteen!' he screamed. 'Quite a load!'

Her speed gradually increased and her exhaust became noticeably softer. Escaping steam from a leaking heating pipe drifted across the track, and she was quickly lost in a haze of steam and smoke.

York shed possessed a large allocation of 'B16' 4-6-0s, and these continually popped up on all sorts of traffic. A good robust design, Philip called them – workmanlike. Other former LNER classes were also represented – 'B1s', 'V2s', 'K3s' and 'J39s' appeared, together with ex-LMS Stanier 8Fs, 'Black Fives' and 'Jubilees'.

'A1' Nos 60150 *Willbrook* and 60142 *Edward Fletcher* arrived and departed, followed by 'A3' No 60066 *Merry Hampton*, but as yet no 'A4s'. Where were they?

York had a large allocation of 'B16' mixed-traffic 4-6-0s – a good robust workmanlike design, according to Philip. No 61435 is seen at Hawes with the RCTS 'North Yorkshireman' rail tour on 25 April 1964. *Ray Ruffell, Silver Link Publishing collection*

A smoky panorama of York shed yard on 26 June 1965, photographed from the passing 'Heart of Midlothian' express. *Ray Ruffell, Silver Link Publishing collection*

While waiting to see a 'streak' the boys spotted 'A1' 'Pacifics' Nos 60150 Willbrook and 60142 *Edward Fletcher*. Here's another of the class, No 60162 *Saint Johnstoun*, north of the border at Dunfermline, northbound for Perth and Inverness. *Ray Ruffell, Silver Link Publishing collection*

'"Streak"!' The cry sent a ripple of excitement along the platform, and all heads turned to watch an approaching express. Majestically 'A4' No 60009 *Union of South Africa** glided by on the 'Flying Scotsman'. Cheering drifted on the wind, and leaning out of the cab her Tam o'Shanter-attired fireman gave a 'thumbs-up' sign, intensifying the excitement. In acknowledgement the locomotive tooted twice before rounding the curve north of the station. Silently the trio watched her vanish, a swirling pall of smoke the only reminder of her passing.

Philip stirred. 'She's not as good as a "Semi".' Paul was not so sure.

Designed by Sir Nigel Gresley for the LNER, the streamlined 'A4' Class marked the pinnacle of an outstanding career. In 1938 *Mallard* reached a speed of 126mph, creating a world record for steam and writing her name into the pages of history, a true flyer in every sense. An improvement on the

A 'streak' at York. With steam to spare and still displaying her former LNER Garter blue livery, No 5 *Sir Charles Newton* drifts through York station with the up 'Flying Scotsman' on 20 March 1948. Judging by the apparent lack of interest displayed by the traditionally attired schoolboys one wonders whether they were serious spotters. Perhaps the 'A4' was a 'stink', but a wonderful sight nevertheless. *D. P. Rowlands*

earlier 'A1' and 'A3' classes, they succeeded the former on most of the LNER's prestige Anglo-Scottish expresses.

After copping 'Jubilee' No 45685 *Barfleur* on a Bristol to York express, they ate, Tubby's suggestion meeting with approval. Tunefully Type 4 English Electric diesel No D238 rumbled through as Paul munched a sandwich. Philip eagerly recorded her number, bringing an outburst from his pal.

'Those diesels are getting about, aren't they?' said Paul, looking provocatively at Philip, who remained silent; his pal was trying his patience.

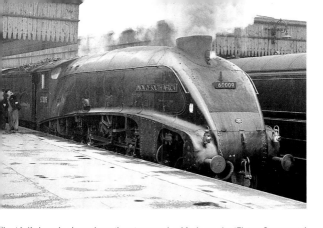

The 'A4' that the boys happily witnessed at York on the 'Flying Scotsman' that day was the majestic No 60009 *Union of South Africa*. Seen here at Aberdeen on the 13.30 'Grampian Express' on 21 June 1965, she was withdrawn almost exactly a year later. Happily she was immediately purchased from BR and has since been very active in preservation. *Ray Ruffell, Silver Link Publishing collection*

Fifteen minutes passed before 'A2' 'Pacific' No 60534 *Irish Elegance* exploded onto the scene, bringing them to their feet. Tubby, in merry mood, gestured at the fleeing locomotive.

'Fancy putting an engine like that on a fish train – seems a little fishy to me!' Groans and hoots went up – surely he could do better that that!

Paul enquired if they fancied going to the Railway Museum. They declined, fearful of what they might miss. This decision coincided with the arrival of 'A4' No 60016 *Silver King*, Paul gleefully copping his Hornby Dublo three-rail engine. A busy period followed during which 'B1' No 61021 *Reitbok*, 'V2' No 60808, 'A1' No 60138 *Boswell*, 'J39' No 64935 and 'Britannia' No 70012 *John of Gaunt* were added to their growing list.

A calm then followed, broken by the sound of a 'Q6' heavy goods engine wheezing along on a heavy coal train. They watched her progress, the jarring of a sticking brake sending shock waves through any onlooker. Her general appearance could only be described as shoddy; grime covered most the locomotive, making her cab number almost indistinguishable. Eyes strained.

'Looks like 63895,' voiced Tubby.

'63395*,' said Paul, correcting his pal.

'They never seem to clean goods engines, do they?' muttered Tubby wistfully.

'No, they don't,' Philip replied. 'The railway's always short of cleaners – it's a rotten job and poorly paid. Still, you've got to start at the bottom of the ladder before you can get on the footplate.'

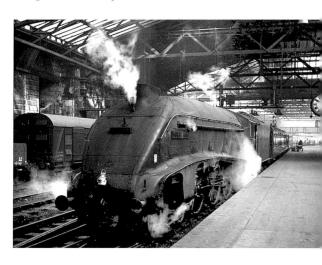

When 'A4' No 60016 *Silver King* arrived, Paul was happy to cop his Hornby Dublo three-rail engine! *Ray Ruffell, Silver Link Publishing collection*

bove: 'A1' No 60138 *Boswell* was another cop, as hopefully it was for the *s*potters on the right of this photograph taken at York on 15 July 1961. *J*hn Corkill

bove: During this busy period 'Britannia' 4-6-2 No 70012 *John of Gaunt* *w*as added to the notebooks. Being inspected by a pair of young spotters, *i*e stands at London Liverpool Street on 2 April 1960. *Frank Hornby*

After the excitement of the 'namers' came a 'Q6' 0-8-0 heavy good
engine wheezing along on a heavy coal train. No 63381 is hauling a trai
of hoppers into Newcastle Central on 22 February 1962. *Ray Ruffell, Silve*
Link Publishing collection

Paul looked distant, as if disturbed.

'Penny for them,' said Tubby, watching his pal. Paul
shook his head and turned to watch 'B1' No 61306*,
seemingly heading for the shed. Philip claiming that most
firemen preferred a 'Black Five' to a 'B1', as they were
easier to fire. Tubby nodded in agreement. Paul thought
the 'B1s' were quite elegant and well-proportioned. Many
carried names, making them welcome additions to his *ABC
Combined*.

The sands of time were rapidly running out, and an
eventful day drew to a close. A Scarborough train arrived
just as they were boarding for Leeds; at its head stood 'D49'
No 62762 *The Fernie*, a member of a class with a reputation
for rough riding, Philip maintained.

Leeds gradually shrank from sight and smoke drifted and
danced across the ever-changing landscape as their train,
hauled by a toiling 'Jubilee', climbed towards Morley Tunnel
At St Helens Junction the compartment door opened and
the guard studied three sleeping figures. He dithered before
deciding against disturbing them – obviously trainspotters

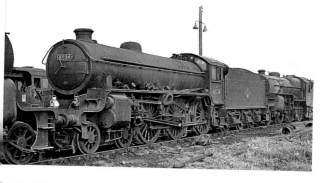

No 61134, seen here, was one of more than 400 'B1' 4-6-0s built for the LNER from 1942. In some ways the LNER's equivalent to the LMS's 'Black Five', Philip claimed that most firemen preferred the Stanier engine. The boys saw No 61306, one of two 'B1s' to be preserved, and now named *Mayflower*. *Ray Ruffell, Silver Link Publishing collection*

udging by their locomotive badges. Smiling, he closed the door. He'd been a spotter himself in his youth. Ah, he vividly recalled trips he'd made to Chester and Crewe. He started to whistle. Good days, he reflected – oh yes, they were good days...

POSTSCRIPT

Although the characters in this story are fictitious, two are loosely based on real personalities. Philip applied for railway service in the early 1960s, as did Paul, both applications meeting with success. Philip soon climbed the promotional ladder, going on to obtain an important managerial position. Paul left British Railways in 1965 after three years, the 'Beeching Plan' motivating his departure. Besides, he'd found a new love, blonde with blue eyes – and who wanted Sundays, anyway? As for Tubby, like the other characters mentioned, he never existed, being merely a figment of my imagination.

GLOSSARY

'Black Five'	Ex-LMS Class 5 4-6-0
'Blink Niner'	BR Standard Class 9F 2-10-0
Bo-Bo	Diesel locomotive with two twin-axle bogies
'Brit'	BR Standard Class 7P 'Britannia' 'Pacific'
Bulleid	Oliver Bulleid, Chief Mechanical Engineer of the Southern Railway, 1937-49
Bunking	Visiting a shed without a permit
'Clan'	BR Standard Class 6P 'Pacific'
'Coffee Pot'/'Super D'	Local nickname for a former LNWR Class 'G1'/'G2' 0-8-0 heavy freight locomotive
Cop	An engine seen for the first time
'Crab'	LMS-designed 2-6-0 mixed-traffic engine with large inclined cylinders
Hornby Dublo	Model railway manufactured by Meccano Ltd, Binns Road, Liverpool
Ian Allan ABC	A small pocket book containing the numbers of steam engines allocated to a particular Region of British Railways, published by Ian Allan Ltd
Ian Allan ABC Combined	A hardback book combining the different regional books and containing the numbers of all steam, diesel and electric locomotives and multiple units operating on British Railways
'Jinty'	Former LMS 0-6-0T shunting engine
'Jub'	Local nickname for 'Jubilee' Class express passenger engine
'Mickey'	Local nickname for a 'Black Five'
Namer	An engine carrying a nameplate
'Pacific'	A steam locomotive with a 4-6-2 wheel arrangement
'Peak'	Diesel-electric locomotive, later Classes 44-46
Peg	Signal; a signal 'pegged' is one in the 'off' ('Clear') position
Picture cop	Photograph of an engine previously seen
'Pug'	Small saddle tank shunting engine
'Semi'	Ex-LMS 'Duchess' 'Pacific', sometimes referred to as 'Coronations'
Standards	Various classes of modern steam engines introduced by British Railways during the 1950s
'Stink'	An engine seen many times before
'Streak'	LNER Gresley 'A4' Class streamlined 'Pacific'
'WD'/'Austerity'	Heavy freight engines introduced during the Second World War